BECOMING
a Better
TEACHER

EIGHT
INNOVATIONS
THAT
WORK

Giselle O. Martin-Kniep

Association for Supervision and Curriculum Development
Alexandria, Virginia USA

Association for Supervision and Curriculum Development
1703 N. Beauregard St. • Alexandria, VA 22311-1714 USA
Telephone: 1-800-933-2723 or 703-578-9600 • Fax: 703-575-5400
Web site: http://www.ascd.org • E-mail: member@ascd.org

Printed in the United States of America.

ASCD Product No. 100043   s11/00
ASCD member price: $18.95   nonmember price: $22.95

Library of Congress Cataloging-in-Publication Data

Martin-Kniep, Giselle O., 1956–
   Becoming a better teacher : eight innovations that work / Giselle O.
Martin-Kniep.
       p. cm.
Includes bibliographical references and index.
"ASCD product no. 100043"—T.p. verso.
ISBN 0-87120-385-5 (alk. paper)
   1. Effective teaching.   2. Curriculum planning.   3. Educational tests
and measurements.   I. Title.
LB1025.3 .M3374 2000
371.102—dc21   00-010673

06 05 04 03 02   10 9 8 7 6 5 4 3

To the teachers who continue to inspire me
Pat, David, Linda, Joanne, Kathy, Ardis, Kim, Angela

To the colleagues who believe in teachers as I do
Diane, Diana, Mark

To those who remind me of what is important
Rick, Nanette, Jean, Carl

To those who know how to shape words
Mark and Jo Ann

and

To Liah, who, despite her absence, is ever present

Contents

Figures

Introduction

Schools are bombarded by good ideas and bad ideas, and even many of the good ideas are poorly implemented. Some of the best innovations die a quick death because not enough is done to institutionalize them. The reasons are not difficult to understand. Educational systems are conservative by design and resistant to change. Many schools lack basic equipment, supplies, and space. Many teachers lack the training and administrative support required to confront a growing number of students with myriad social, emotional, and cognitive needs. Sometimes policy is made without supporting evidence of the validity of the proposed changes. Schools react, initially respond, and eventually become distracted by competing forces and new ideas. Professional development is too often considered a luxury, insufficiently supported by all but a handful of schools and districts throughout the nation.

Many teachers in the United States do not have access to serious professional development after they get their educational degrees. Their induction into schools and subsequent survival depend greatly on the people they work with, the conditions that surround them, and the more experienced peers who mentor them. Teachers who have access to professional development fare better than those who don't, inasmuch as they learn about educational innovations and are given the tools to incorporate them into their teaching practices. However, without a supportive administrative staff and continued feedback on their use of these innovations, teachers tend to abandon any innovation that distances them too much from the status quo in their schools.

This book is about good innovations well worth implementing. It is aimed at teachers and administrators who may have had little formal exposure to them and who want to consider their implementation. It is also suitable for teachers who have been exposed to some aspects of learner-centered education but have had few opportunities to link these into a coherent whole. I chose the eight innovations discussed in this book because, as a whole, they foster a student-centered classroom environment that is both equitable and rigorous. Each of the innovations has a long history of implementation and has been researched and evaluated in a variety of settings. Some of them have been the subject of one or more professional books, but I do not know of any book in print that examines several innovations in one convenient presentation.

My decision to do so stems from a belief that these innovations are necessary, but individually they are not sufficient to enhance student learning. In fact, one of the problems in professional development workshops and conferences is that these innovations are treated as self-contained ideas and techniques that are divorced from a supportive context. For example, workshops on rubrics or assessment do not sufficiently account for the fact that rubrics and performance assessments need to be attached to curriculum assignments and learning experiences. Similarly, it makes no sense for teachers to develop portfolios for students if they do not provide students with worthy assignments for their portfolio collections and with ongoing opportunities for students to reflect on their learning. Many teacher workshops are not long enough to include time to link the use of portfolios with the kinds of assignments that are likely to enhance their use.

Although I have written this book for teachers who have little prior knowledge of the innovations described, more experienced teachers can also benefit from reviewing these innovations and considering them as parts of a comprehensive whole. It is difficult for teachers to nurture true learning if they don't experience the learning process for themselves.

In addition, I urge teachers to pursue in-depth experiences with any one of the topics addressed in this book. The eight innovations included in this book are (1) essential questions, (2) curriculum integration, (3) standards-based curriculum and assessment design, (4) authentic assessment, (5) scoring rubrics, (6) portfolios, (7) reflection, and (8) action research. The chapters that discuss

the innovations are similar in structure in that they include a rationale, a description of what the innovation requires and what it looks like in different classroom settings, and an overview of the steps teachers can take in incorporating it into their practice. Each chapter is also driven by an essential question and is supported by work samples from teachers and by composite images that allow teachers in grades K–12 to make sense of the material presented. Annotated lists of recommended resources for further learning appear at the end of the chapters.

Chapter 1 tackles the essential question, What is essential? It showcases the use of essential questions as a means to increase classroom discourse and thinking, as a tool for creating curriculum coherence, and as a vehicle for helping students realize that learning is an endless journey—that is, the more we know, the more we know what we have yet to learn. The chapter addresses the following guiding questions: What are essential questions? What do they look like? How can teachers use them? When should teachers use them? How are they different from guiding questions? Who should generate them? How do we assess curriculum that is supported by essential questions? It is no accident that this is the first chapter of the book. The topic makes the statement that substantive inquiry around important questions is intrinsic to a valuable educational experience.

Chapter 2 deals with the need to integrate the curriculum so that teachers and students experience it as a coherent whole rather than as a smorgasbord of isolated activities. It tackles the essential question, Is all integration good? This chapter lays the foundation for integrated curriculum and assessment design and provides teachers with critical background information for making important design decisions. As is the case with many other innovations, attempts at integrating the curriculum are often poorly thought out and too superficial to be good for students or worth the time it takes to put them together. This chapter provides reasons for curricular integration, offers guidelines for the selection and use of organizing centers, suggests criteria for judging the merits of integrated units, and raises important issues related to the development of units at the elementary and secondary levels.

Chapter 3 addresses standards-based curriculum and assessment design. Politicians and educators alike consider standards to be necessary for the attainment of a better education for students. But the standards movement lacks models of practice—that is, specific strategies that help practitioners use such standards to make sound curriculum, instruction, and assessment decisions. Teachers are currently ill-equipped to design student-centered and standards-based constructivist curriculum and assessments and have few opportunities to determine what part of their curriculum is essential and what is redundant or obsolete. This chapter tackles the essential question, What is the best way to package learning? and seeks to provide teachers with practical ideas for addressing the demands posed by district, state, and national standards. It helps teachers graphically represent their curriculum and use this representation as a basis for identifying learner outcomes and relating them to outside standards. It also helps teachers "unpack" standards so they can use them to establish educational priorities for their students.

Chapter 4 highlights the use of authentic assessment and is driven by the question, Can learning in school be authentic? Authentic assessment has been advocated since the mid-1980s as a means to help students engage with real or plausible problems and challenges. Yet most school programs are not conducive to authentic learning experiences.

In fact, one could argue that schools themselves, especially high schools, are designed to minimize authenticity. After all, how many of us experience life in 42-minute segments? This chapter defines the attributes of authentic assessment and shows teachers what it might look like to refine existing assessments to make them more authentic. It provides examples of authentic assessments and guidelines for when and how to design them in different contexts.

Chapter 5 follows naturally from the preceding chapter by exploring the use of scoring rubrics to support and measure learning. The essential question for the chapter is this: How do we communicate what we mean by "good"? Many states, districts, and classroom teachers are now using scoring rubrics to evaluate student learning. However, little has been said about the role of rubrics as scaffolding and supporting tools for learning. This chapter identifies quality indicators of rubrics, helps teachers assess existing rubrics, shows exemplary rubrics, and provides various strategies for developing rubrics with and without student input.

Chapter 6 is about the use of student portfolios as windows into students' thinking and learning. It is supported by the question, Who are we as learners? It argues for portfolios as the most comprehensive tool for documenting students' growth, efforts, and achievements in one or more areas. Portfolios provide evolving images of students' work and, accompanied by students' reflections, enable readers to witness what students think about themselves as learners. This chapter describes different kinds and uses of student portfolios. It provides teachers with guidelines for initiating the use of portfolios and helps them use portfolios as communication tools with parents and other teachers.

Chapter 7 addresses the topic of reflection as a means for teachers to develop a greater understanding of their students and to help them become self-regulated learners. It is supported by the essential question, How do we learn? The chapter is guided by the belief that if we want students to become thoughtful individuals who can assume responsibility for their own learning, we have to teach them how to analyze and evaluate their work. We have to help them define realistic yet challenging goals for their continued learning and show them how to identify appropriate strategies for attaining those goals. The chapter provides various strategies to help students become reflective and shows what student reflection looks like in various grades.

Chapter 8 addresses the topic of action research and answers the following question: How do questions teach? Action research is about asking questions and identifying problems that can be solved through systematic inquiry. It is about believing that we, as teachers, can produce valuable knowledge about our work. This chapter shows teachers what action research requires and provides a step-by-step

process so that they can begin to use it in their practice. It also describes various action research studies conducted by educators in different settings.

The final chapter in this book is about putting all the pieces together. It tackles the following question: What does it look like to be a learner-centered teacher? To fully implement all the preceding innovations, teachers need to embrace certain beliefs about themselves and their work, some of which run contrary to common teaching practices. They need to assume responsibility for the design and implementation of their curriculum instead of seeing themselves simply as implementors of school, district, or state mandates. They need to focus their attention on students' learning and not on what they should cover from day to day. They need to assume a long-term view toward improving their practice and redesigning their curriculum and take short steps that lead them in that direction. This chapter provides teachers with beginning steps for embracing these beliefs.

The Power of Essential Questions

1

[**Essential Question:**
What Is Essential?

One of the things that makes school a chore for so many students is that much of what is taught seems senseless, devoid of any meaningful context. The pressures teachers feel to "cover" the curriculum or to prepare students for standardized tests result in a curriculum that is content-driven rather than learner-based. It is difficult to mediate the needs of the students while attending to the pressures of the text, which is still the most common curriculum organizer. Texts are logical, organized, crisp, and in black and white. Students' needs and backgrounds, on the other hand, are extraordinarily diverse and complex. If the goal is efficiency, the text and the formal curriculum will prevail. The exception to this rule occurs in kindergarten and preschool education, mostly because young children's readiness to respond as passive learners is very limited. The situation changes quickly with socialization pressures and with a curriculum that is too often divorced from students' needs and backgrounds. In many grades and subjects, it is uncommon to find a coherent, learner-based curriculum.

Teachers can use essential questions to engage students with the curriculum. These questions allow teachers to tackle the curriculum while helping them treat it as something to be discovered and negotiated. Essential questions can remind teachers and students that learning is a journey, that the quest to know is never-ending, and that the voyage can begin at any point in time. Essential questions can raise the level of discourse in a classroom by enabling everyone to question and investigate, to discuss and to debate. They can also provide the glue for a unit or a series of lessons, and they can respect the many new tests mandated as a result of new, often more demanding standards.

Essential questions are compelling. They transcend cultural and age boundaries in ways that no other questions do. They are universal. They are never fully answerable. The more individuals grow and mature, the more they know about how much they have yet to learn about such questions. Essential questions sometimes do not appear essential. Their answer appears obvious at first, as with the question *How far is far?* However, as the pondering begins, it becomes clear that the answer is not simple at all, but rather subject to multiple perspectives and interpretations. Essential questions lead to the realization that knowledge is an ongoing search, and one that makes life worth living.

The question of who should generate essential questions suggests various possibilities. Teachers can generate essential questions individually or as a school faculty. Students can also generate essential questions either by themselves or with the teacher.

What Do Essential Questions Look Like?

The following are some examples of essential questions. Units driven by these questions can result in powerful discussions and challenging projects.

- Are we really free?
- Are leaders made or are they born with leadership qualities?
- What is the meaning of life?
- Does history really repeat itself?
- Where does perception end and reality begin?
- How far is far?
- Is there such a thing as a selfless act?
- Is time an absolute thing?
- What makes writing worth reading?
- Is it better to live with the question or the wrong answer?

- How do we explain the unexplainable?
- What is essential?
- What is progress?
- Do we have control over our destiny?
- What's the point of a point of view?
- Is there anything original?
- If we are so alike, how do we explain our differences?
- Can there be good without evil?
- Can a child be a scientist?
- Are humans inhumane?
- What is justice?
- Do people really rule?
- Can a moral person be immoral?
- Are all cultures equally valuable?
- Which culture is best?
- What is happiness?
- Does technology drive new technology or do people drive new technology?
- Is technology invented or discovered?
- Is love at first sight love?
- Can a virtue be a vice?
- What makes art great?
- What is good poetry?
- Who should define what art is?
- Does art change society?
- When does loyalty become cowardice?
- Can you win and lose at the same time?
- Are there any absolutes?
- Are all teachers learners?
- What is worth teaching?
- What is worth testing?
- What is worth learning?
- Of the things that make a good employee, what is teachable?
- What is good parenting?
- When is cheating not bad?
- Is education essential for success in life?

How Might Essential Questions Be Used?

As with the remaining chapters in this book, this chapter begins with a question (*What is essential?*) that provides a framework for the chapter. In the classroom, essential questions can frame a unit, a course, or a year. They can be used to hook students into an inquiry that they will conduct themselves. A question for a yearlong study could be *What makes me who I am?* or *What is progress?* Many of the questions listed in the preceding section lend themselves to specific units of study. What follows are some examples of how these kinds of questions can relate to different content and become the organizing centers of inquiry-driven units.

What is the most important discovery of the 20th century? can launch a unit in which groups of students research a specific discovery, write a position paper, and submit it to *Life* magazine with a proposal for including it in an upcoming issue on innovations worth remembering as the new century begins.

How does art reflect the health of a society? can be used in a unit in which 10th graders visit an art gallery or museum and interview five visitors about what the art exhibit communicates about society. After compiling this information, the students can use it to develop a class-generated letter to the National Endowment for the Arts recommending a specific stance on the funding for specific kinds of work.

The question *When is the cost of discovery too high?* can serve as the springboard to a study of the ethics of cloning in a high school biology class.

Can we have a family of one? can lead a kindergarten class in exploring the concept of family.

Is war a necessity? can frame a middle school unit on the Civil War.

Essential questions can easily be related to standards. Consider the following examples:

• New York State standard: Students will understand mathematics and become mathematically confident by communicating and reasoning mathematically, by applying mathematics in real-world settings, and by solving problems through the integrated study of number systems, geometry, algebra, data analysis, probability, and trigonometry.

Possible essential questions: *What of mathematics is essential? Are numbers real?*

• Florida standard: The student understands the role of the citizen in the American democracy.

Possible essential questions: *Do people really rule? Is the civil rights movement over?*

How Can Essential Questions Be Used in Assessment?

Essential questions can become one of the tools that teachers use to assess students' learning in a unit of study. Teachers can use them as a diagnostic assessment if they ask the question before beginning a specific unit, and they can use them as a summative assessment if they ask students the same question at the end of the unit or if they have students review and revise the answer they gave to the question at the beginning of the unit. Thus, even if the question is never completely answered, teachers can bring the unit to closure by allowing students to assess their growth in understanding from the beginning to the end of the unit.

For example, Rick Hinrichs, a 6th grade teacher in Mattituck, New York, asked his students the following question on pre- and post-tests for a unit on ancient Egypt: Does Egypt qualify as a great civilization? Here is the complete pretest response of one of his students:

> Yes, I think that Egypt qualifies as a great civilization because they had pyramids,

which they used as tombs, lots of sand, which they traveled across; they had elephants which they rode, and the queen, Cleopatra who was very powerful. All these things have to do with civilization.

Here are excerpts from the post-test response of the same student:

> I think that Egypt qualifies as a great civilization because they had a very strong government. They had pharaohs that made rules that the people had to follow. . . . The Ancient Egyptian government was kind of like the US Government. The pharaoh was like the president, and he had people to help him make laws . . .
>
> To be civilized you also need a language. If you have a language you are able to talk, write, and learn. Ancient Egyptian writing was called Hieroglyphics. . . .
>
> You also need a Religion. Egyptians believed in many gods. . . .
>
> Ancient Egyptians had a culture, a way of life. But almost every man had to help build the Pyramid that the pharaoh of that time would be put in when he died. The main people that built the pyramids were farmers and slaves because they made up most of the Egyptian population. . . .
>
> Since scribes made many records, a lot of them were found in later years, . . . All the records were written on Papyrus. Papyrus was made of reeds from the delta in the mouth of the Nile River.
>
> Along the sides of the Nile River there was very rich soil. The soil was so rich because every year when the Nile River overflowed. When the water level came back down Silt had been deposited on the riverbanks. . . . The rich soil parts were full of plants because they grew very well there. People planted plants in the middle of the desert too. Since the plants needed to be

watered, Egyptians needed Irrigation. This included wells and canals.

> All these things have to do with why I think that Ancient Egypt was civilized. . . .

The differences in the student's responses on the pre- and post-test to the same essential question clearly demonstrate growth in learning. For a rubric used to assess such an essential question, please see the rubric in Figure 5.10 (p. 50).

Why Ask Essential Questions?

Educators should ask essential questions because there are times when it is important for students to ponder universal issues, to do substantive research that is more than the mere gathering of facts, to learn that the world of ideas is complex and that sometimes many different and equally valid ways of interpreting the same event or issue apply. Without asking essential questions, what is there for education to do? Essential questions should be at the heart of learning within and outside schools.

How Do Essential Questions Differ from Guiding Questions?

Essential questions are not meant to elicit a "right" or "wrong" answer; they are meant to be addressed, to prompt students to think expansively, to consider ideas. They are universal and do not belong to a specific subject. Guiding questions, also known as unit questions, stem from a specific curriculum. They are objectives turned into questions. For example, the objective "Students will identify the topographic characteristics of Japan" can become the guiding question "What are the topographic characteristics of Japan?"

Some examples of guiding questions that stem from the question *What is the most important discovery of the 20th century?* are these: How did the invention of the telephone change society? How has our ability to map the human genome affected our ability to extend life? The essential question *Is war a necessity?* could be supported by the following guiding questions: Who were the main decision makers during the Civil War? What are the various justifications for that war? Who were the losers? Who were the winners?

Whereas only one essential question drives a unit, many guiding questions support it.

When Are Essential Questions Appropriate?

Teachers should use essential questions to launch an inquiry-based unit in which they do not feel compelled to provide students with the one right answer. Essential questions work best when supporting a unit integrated around broad concepts, such as war, justice, community, tradition, interdependence, systems, power, and light. They are harder to develop, but just as important, for units that are driven by narrower topics, such as *Hamlet*, the Civil War, or China. Essential questions should not be asked when a unit involves no inquiry—that is, when the teacher has a specific body of information to deliver without any questioning or research by students. The following are some criteria for the development of essential questions.

1. *Teachers should be comfortable with not answering the question.* The main purposes for using essen-

tial questions are to help students ponder issues or ideas that are intrinsically complex and to realize that the search for knowledge is ongoing and does not end when a unit or course is over. The question may literally be answered, but everyone will recognize that even a very thoughtful and carefully prepared answer is not the only possible answer to an essential question. Some answers, of course, may be more persuasive than others.

2. *Everyone should relate to the question.* A question is essential if people of all ages, ethnicities, and backgrounds find it important. However, the universal nature of essential questions does not mean that the material that supports them is equally accessible to all students. Teachers should ensure that the material is relevant and significant for specific groups of students.

3. *The question should be congruent with the unit content.* The unit or course needs to provide students with enough material and content for them to be able to understand the question at a much deeper level. They should have more to say about possible answers at the end of the unit than when they first asked themselves the question.

4. *The question should be realistic and teachable in the context of the time and the course or grade taught.* The question needs to be approachable within the time and resources available during the unit.

5. *The question should elicit multiple perspectives.* The question should be accompanied by opportunities for students to explore different viewpoints or approaches to the question.

6. *The question should generate as many questions as it answers.* Ending the unit with many more questions than the students had when they began the unit shows that they have attained a deeper understanding of the question and its implications. The adage "The more we know the more we know what we don't know" applies here.

Activities for the Reader

1. Create one or two guiding questions for one of the following essential questions:

    a. Are some stereotypes true?
    b. Should all citizens be treated equally?
    c. Can/should change be stopped?

2. Generate an essential question for an inquiry-based unit you plan to teach. Use the criteria in this chapter to assess whether you have an essential question or a guiding question.

Recommended Resources

Jacobs, H. H. (1997). *Mapping the big picture: Integrating the curriculum and assessment K–12*. Alexandria, VA: Association for Supervision and Curriculum Development.
This is an easy-to-read, practical, concise handbook for any district interested in developing a map of their K–12 programs integrating curriculum and assessment. A helpful chapter discusses how to develop and write essential questions to frame or guide curricular design. The book helps to put essential questions into the context of the larger actual curriculum of a teacher, school, or school district.

Jacobs outlines seven steps (phases) districts can follow when creating and working with curriculum maps based on the school calendar year. Readers are asked to review, analyze, and develop curriculum maps specific to their own disciplines based on what they actually teach. Curriculum mapping provides a visual to identify potential gaps in instruction, redundancies, and possible areas for integration. The book includes examples of schools and teachers who have implemented curriculum mapping. Appendixes provide sample curriculum maps and examples of essential questions.

Wiggins, G., & McTighe, J. (1998). *Understanding by design*. Alexandria, VA: Association for Supervision and Curriculum Development.
This book introduces readers to a backward curriculum design process that emphasizes depth, rigor, and understanding. The authors refer to essential and unit questions in several of the chapters and include numerous examples of essential questions throughout the book.

Curriculum Integration as a Tool for Coherence

2

[
Essential Question:
Is All Integration Good?

In many classrooms, teachers feel they have too much to do and too little time to teach everything students need to know. Textbooks and supplementary resources continue to grow in response to an increased knowledge base. In addition, an increasing number of district, state, and national demands impinge on teachers' use of classroom time. On the other hand, students' needs have not diminished. Human problems, especially those of children and adolescents, are best dealt with through intense and continuous one-on-one communication and through healthy interactions that enable adults to become positive role models and guides. Such communication is increasingly difficult to come by given the ever-growing compartmentalization of the school day.

Having too much to teach with increasingly thicker and more demanding textbooks presents a challenge. It makes it difficult for teachers to carefully consider the relationships between seemingly unconnected materials from within and across subjects. Much of what students experience as they move from one class to another and from one subject to another is unconnected to a larger whole. It is therefore imperative to find ways to consolidate content so that students and teachers can make sense of the myriad stimuli that affect them.

Teachers need to assume greater control of the local curriculum by designing and implementing a limited number of integrated units and lessons instead of relying primarily on textbooks and teaching isolated activities and lessons. The overall principle to keep in mind is *coherence*. Curriculum integration can be a critical means for developing coherence in students' learning experiences.

This chapter presents reasons for curriculum integration, describes three different kinds of curriculum integration, provides guidelines for the selection and use of organizing centers, suggests criteria for judging the validity of integrated units, and raises important issues to consider in the development of units at the elementary and secondary levels. Chapter 3 goes through the steps to design an integrated, standards-based unit. This chapter provides the background and guidelines teachers need to understand before they can build a practical unit with curriculum integrity. Although this chapter is short, the cautions and guideposts are many. They are not meant to constitute a fixed template and need not be slavishly followed. They are meant to give teachers a feeling for what is at stake and generally how to proceed.

What Are the Reasons for Curriculum Integration?

Curriculum integration calls for the development of connections between sometimes natural and sometimes seemingly disparate bodies of knowledge and skills, and between students' experiences and backgrounds and what they learn in school. The primary reasons propelling curriculum integration are (1) growing support for learning and assessment experiences that require the application of knowledge rather than memorization and accumulation of facts; (2) increasing understanding of how the brain processes information through patterns and connections with an emphasis on coherence; (3) emerging awareness that knowledge is neither fixed nor universal, and that problems of real significance cannot be solved out of a single discipline of knowledge; and (4) the belief that an integrated curriculum can help teachers and students overcome rigid and arbitrary perceptions of subject boundaries. For more than 70 years, philosophers, researchers, and educators have questioned the validity of separate subject approaches to curriculum

(Wrightstone, 1935, 1936; Informal committee of the Progressive Education Association, 1941; Aikin, 1942; Hanna & Lang, 1950; Soodak & Martin-Kniep, 1994). These reviews indicate that students' learning is enhanced as the curriculum moves further in the direction of integration.

What Are the Forms of Curriculum Integration?

Curriculum integration can appear in various forms. Integration of content refers to connections of the content within and among subjects. A social studies teacher's use of art or literature to enable students to develop a broader understanding of a cultural region is an example of content integration within a classroom. A social studies teacher and an English teacher teaching a jointly developed unit on culture that blurs the boundaries between the two subjects is an example of content integration across subjects. Both of these forms of content integration are also referred to as interdisciplinary curriculum.

Integration of skills involves connections among skills and processes and the contexts in which they apply (that is, reading, writing, and thinking across the curriculum). Integration of school and self concerns connections between what goes on in school and the students' outside world, including their desires, experiences, aspirations, and interests (Case, 1991).

Each of these forms of integration has a rightful place in the classroom and requires purposeful and strategic decisions by teachers. This chapter addresses the integration of content and skills and how such integration relates to curriculum design. Chapter 7 addresses the topic of reflection, which is one of the most useful ways to promote the integration of students' selves and their learning.

What Are Organizing Centers?

The organizing center is the hub of the unit—what holds it together. There are many kinds of organizing centers, including topics (the American Revolution, African Americans), themes (bears, aviation), concepts (war, change, flight), phenomena and problems (deforestation in Brazil, violence in schools), and issues (human rights, immigration into the United States).

Several authors offer various classifications for organizing centers. These classifications can help teachers assess the relative merits of some organizing centers over others. For example, Beane (1997) classifies organizing centers into the following categories: (1) topics contained within the separate subjects (Colonial living, myths and legends, the Middle Ages), (2) social problems or issues (conflict, the environment, education), (3) issues and concerns of young people (getting along with peers, life in school, Who am I?), (4) appealing topics (dinosaurs, apples, teddy bears), and (5) process-oriented topics (change, systems, cycles).

On the other hand, Willard Kniep (1979) identifies four kinds of organizing centers that can, in turn, become unit themes: (1) processes of inquiry, (2) concepts, (3) phenomena, and (4) persistent problems. Process-based themes result in skill-building units that focus on the ways that social scientists solve problems and investigate reality. Process-based units include observing, gathering data, establishing comparisons, and making models. Such units can sometimes be taught as prerequisites of concept- and problem-based units. For example, a teacher might teach a unit on observation and classification before launching a unit on mass media that requires students to conduct independent research and collect data.

Concept-based units are designed to provide students with mental structures they can use to describe the world they live in. Examples include cause/effect relationships, community, culture, change, family, motivation, population, scarcity, systems, supply and demand, technology, and values. A concept-based unit focused on the family might be guided by the essential question *Can you have a family of one?* and might require that students explore different kinds of family units and configurations across generations and cultures and in the arts.

Phenomenon-based units enable students to understand the world around them. Examples include banks, communities, economic systems, families, governments, groups, landforms, literature, media, oceans, political organizations, religions, and wars. A unit centered on economic systems might ask students to analyze different economic systems at the micro and macro levels; to explore the relationships among technological, economic, and political systems; and to investigate the social, cultural, and psychological implications of different economic arrangements.

Units centered on persistent problems enable students to understand persistent world problems and to apply what they know to possible solutions for those problems. An example of such a unit would be the current depletion of the rain forest, whereby students would investigate the rain forest as a problem that affects multiple and diverse peoples and systems.

Some organizing centers—conflict and war, for example—can be categorized as a concept, a phenomenon, or a persistent problem. However, the learning experiences and assessments that teachers select help define the use of the organizing center within a unit so that it can be appropriately placed within one of these categories.

According to Boyer (1995), organizing centers should be selected as they pertain to the human commonalities that contribute to the educated person. These commonalities include the life cycle, language, the arts, time and space, groups and institutions, work, the natural world, and the search for meaning.

Regardless of the classification and choice of centers for a unit, the organizing center should provide the context for unifying the knowledge and skills in a unit. In turn, the content and skills within a unit become critical to students' understanding of the organizing center.

What Considerations Affect Selection of an Organizing Center?

Some organizing centers are better than others for anchoring lessons and supporting inquiry. Concepts, problems, and issues tend to be more generative than themes and topics. A generative center, such as the concept of war, allows for better and more interdisciplinary connections and real-life applications than a less generative center, such as the topic of the Civil War in the United States. Thus, one of the considerations for selecting an organizing center should be the extent to which it is generative and can enable teachers to address multiple outcomes and standards, as well as content from different subjects that are naturally related to each other. According to Beane (1997), organizing centers that are not related to significant self and social issues are not appropriate for curriculum integration.

When selecting an organizing center, teachers should ask themselves the following questions:

• Will this center be recognized as important by people of different genders, races, and cultures?

• Will this center be as timely and relevant 5 or 10 years from now as it is today?

• Is this center equally appropriate and central to all the subjects and disciplines that the unit will incorporate?

• Is this center equally appropriate for students in different grade levels?

• Does this center support the use of critical information about a theme, issue, or problem?

• Does this center foster the exploration of a theme, issue, or problem from different disciplinary venues?

• Does this center create the possibility for students to make important generalizations about what they learn?

What Criteria Can Be Used to Judge the Merits and Validity of Integrated Units?

Having a generative and significant organizing center is a necessary but not sufficient condition for developing a valid unit. As teachers develop an integrated curriculum unit, they need to determine the unit's validity by applying at least three other important criteria: (1) significance or meaningfulness, (2) relevance, and (3) cohesiveness or coherence.

The first criterion, significance or meaningfulness, refers to the substance of the lessons within the unit and of the unit itself. It seeks to determine if the lessons and unit address important content in the subject areas addressed. To apply this criterion, teachers could ask themselves the following questions:

• Are the concepts addressed by the unit important for all the disciplines involved?

• Is the unit likely to help students better understand a specific discipline-based concept or idea because it has been dealt with in an interdisciplinary fashion?

• Is the material in the unit so important that it transcends discipline-based boundaries?

• Does the unit enhance students' learning processes?

The second criterion, relevance, concerns the extent to which the material and strategies used to present the lessons in the unit allow students to make meaningful cognitive or affective connections. Framed as a question, the criterion asks, Can students relate personally to the material and the delivery strategies used to teach that material?

The last criterion, cohesiveness or coherence, concerns the extent to which the activities within the lessons and the unit itself are closely linked and articulated to provide a tight fit between them. It also concerns the extent to which the instructional strategies used are consistent with the lesson objectives and unit outcomes.

What Issues Should Be Considered When Exploring Curriculum Integration?

Regardless of the grade or subject taught, all teachers should consider the following issues:

• *Validity of material.* All material and units should meet every test and standard the teachers normally bring to anything they teach.

• *Current curricular strengths and weaknesses.* Teachers should select organizing centers and develop units that are consistent with their own curricular strengths and interests.

• *Perceived curricular needs.* The first units to be developed should be those that fill an existing gap in the curriculum.

• *Current programmatic strengths and weaknesses.* Some programs are naturally conducive to and supportive of specific units and centers (that is, schools that have humanities departments instead of separate social studies, art, and English departments can best support humanities-oriented units; schools where teachers are grouped into teams who teach the same groups of students in 80-minute blocks are better able to implement integrated units).

• *Awareness of present curricular scope and sequence, and amount of curriculum slack.* Units do not exist in isolation. They are situated in specific contexts in which important content precedes and follows them. It is important to remember the need to build horizontal relationships (across content) without sacrificing vertical relationships (across time).

• *Opportunities for faculty to explore curricula.* The development of integrated units is most effective when teachers have the opportunity to behave as learners and explorers as well as designers.

Curricular integration presents significant challenges to teachers. At the elementary level, teachers must have enough understanding of the disciplines they teach to allow thoughtful considerations of the possible and natural relationships among those disciplines. This is difficult for the many elementary teachers who are generalists, with depth of knowledge in only one or two disciplines other than reading and social studies. Both elementary and secondary teachers face the additional challenge of having to know how to use the experiential and learner-centered pedagogical strategies necessary for the exploration of relationships, concepts, and insights that are prevalent in solid integrated units. This is contrary to prevailing instructional practices that emphasize teacher-dominated talk. At the secondary level, teachers face the challenges of rigid structures that make team teaching, collaborative planning, and back-to-back scheduling difficult; in addition, they sometimes suffer from lack of administrative support.

Notwithstanding the challenges, the integration of curriculum is a worthwhile and important goal. The next chapter describes the process teachers can use to accomplish it.

What Is the Process for Developing Integrated Units?

Integrated units can be developed by individual teachers or by two or more teachers of different subjects who share the same students. Individual teachers can follow the design process outlined in Chapter 3. Teachers sharing students can amend that process by following these steps:

1. Each teacher within a group identifies two learner outcomes for his or her course or subject. One of the outcomes should refer to something that students should be able to do; the other should address something important (a concept or key idea) that students should know. The group consolidates all outcomes listed.

2. The group brainstorms potential organizing centers that would address as many learner outcomes as are on the list and selects a center that best meets the criteria of substantiveness, generalizability, relevance, and so on.

3. The group identifies one essential question for that organizing center, with supporting guiding questions.

4. The group identifies a culminating authentic assessment.

5. The group brainstorms potential activities within different subject areas and skill domains using a web.

6. The group selects activities for the unit and sketches them in pencil, starting from the authentic assessment and working backward to the beginning of the unit. When sketching, the group identifies lessons and assessments for each day.

Recommended Resources

Beane, J. A. (1997). *Curriculum integration: Designing the core of democratic education*. New York: Columbia University, Teachers College Press.
The author asks educators to look back to curriculum integration as the root of progressive education in the 1920s and '30s. He argues that we can apply knowledge to questions and concerns that have personal and social significance in the common world by organizing curriculum in specific ways. He establishes that the difference between integrated curriculum and multidisciplinary or interdisciplinary curriculum is that the latter distinctly separates classical subjects and fragments learning. Integrated curriculum, on the other hand, raises questions about common social issues, using concepts and learned skills as tools to tie knowledge together, and uses a hierarchy of thinking to solve a problem.

Egan, K. (1986). *Teaching as story telling*. Chicago: University of Chicago Press.
Egan offers an alternative to the generally accepted elementary school curriculum that begins with the concrete and builds toward the abstract. After questioning some of the educational principles on which the typical curriculum is based, Egan suggests instead an elementary school curriculum based on what he calls "The Great Stories of the World Curriculum." He suggests teachers use his Story Form Model, which begins with questions such as "What is most important about this topic?" "Why should it matter to children?" "What is effectively engaging about this topic?" "What binary opposites best catch the importance of this topic?" and "What content most dramatically embodies the binary opposites, in order to provide access to the topic?"

Ellis, Arthur K., & Stuen, Carol J. (1998). *The interdisci-
     plinary curriculum*. Raleigh, NC: Eye on Education.
This book includes chapters on the nature of knowledge, components of the inquiry process, concept formation, and reflective thinking. The authors also address
issues such as integration of subject matter and aca-
demic integrity, the importance of major themes, and
the role of experience in learning. The authors offer
classroom-tested examples and models of interdisciplinary curriculum at different grade levels and involving
different subjects.

Jensen, E. (1998). *Teaching with the brain in mind*.
     Alexandria, VA: Association for Supervision and
     Curriculum Development.
The author gives a rather detailed overview of various
aspects of brain research, including learning and the two
hemispheres of the brain; sleep time for middle and high
school students; food for the brain, not just for muscle
growth; how enrichment for all students (not only gifted
and talented) can make the brain better; the link between emotions and learning and between movement
and learning; and how memory works. The author emphasizes the need to understand that today's students are
not necessarily different from students years ago; they
just learn differently; and that current brain research
must focus more on educational implications.

Wiggins, G., & McTighe, J. (1998). *Understanding by
     design*. Alexandria, VA: Association for Supervision
     and Curriculum Development.
Teachers would agree that, whatever the content, their
goal is that students will understand a concept or
process. But what is understanding? The authors explain
six facets of understanding. They propose a "backward
design" model; after determining what students need to
know and be able to do, teachers should design the assessments that show evidence of this understanding.
Readers are taken through this design process and given
classroom examples as well as design templates. Issues of
constructivism, conceptual change, and "uncoverage"
naturally arise in the discussion. Although useful to the
classroom teacher, this book would be of considerable interest to any professional involved in curriculum design.

Standards-Based Curriculum and Assessment Design

3

[
Essential Question:
What Is the Best Way to
Package Learning?
]

The logic behind using standards as the foundation for curriculum, instruction, and assessment is compelling. First, schools, like most other organizations, need to pay at least as much attention to the quality of what they produce, namely graduates—as they do to the processes and content involved. In fact, that is the primary logic behind national and state standards efforts. Second, curriculum content and teacher expectations for students in the same courses and grade levels vary greatly within and across buildings, districts, and states. Although there is no question that teachers need the freedom to teach in different ways to best meet the needs of students, it is difficult to justify that a teacher in one 1st grade classroom can define reading as having students memorize five words per week, while a 1st grade teacher across the hallway has students reading books of all genres

throughout the week. Finally, teachers' grading practices vary within and across grade levels. This variability could be greatly decreased if schools had a shared understanding of and commitment to the same standards and benchmarks.

The standards movement lacks models of practice—that is, of specific strategies that help practitioners use such standards to make sound decisions about curriculum, instruction, and assessment. This chapter presents a standards-based curriculum and assessment design process that can help teachers develop or refine their curriculum in ways that are aligned with their own exit outcomes and with district, state, or national standards.

The design process described in this chapter is comprehensive and labor-intensive. It involves the development of a limited number of integrated curriculum units with accompanying assessments that encompass required district, state, and national standards. It requires a fair amount of teacher effort and thought. Obviously, teachers will not be able to design everything they teach with great care, given the time constraints posed by their school-year demands. This process assumes that teachers are given time during the year and in the summer to design one or more integrated units, either individually or as a team. It also presupposes that teachers will devise a long-term strategy for curriculum design, tinkering with 10 to 20 percent of their curriculum yearly and planning to revamp or redesign their entire curriculum over a five- to seven-year period.

Before developing a standards-based unit with accompanying assessments, it is important that teachers generate a list or a visual representation of the components of their subject or grade-level curriculum. This task involves listing, webbing, or graphing the concepts, skills, texts, assessments, topics, and outcomes it includes. The curriculum components would be different for elementary, middle, secondary, and special area teachers. What matters is that before committing to the design of one or more multiweek units, teachers have a sense of their year as a whole so they can see how this unit fits into the whole plan.

Figure 3.1 is a list that Rick Hinrichs—a 6th grade teacher in the Mattituck School District in Long Island, New York—developed for his social studies curriculum.

The curriculum design process described here has many possible points of departure. Some teachers begin the design process by defining learner outcomes for students and then designing a unit to meet them. Figure 3.2 on page 18 shows this particular approach to the design process and lists questions that teachers can ask as they build their curriculum units.

When and How Are Standards-Based Units Designed?

Because standards-based units require considerable planning and organization, they are best developed when teachers have a block of time available for design—during the summer, for example, or a combination of vacation time, release time during the school year, and after-school meetings.

The design process is recursive; it occurs every time the teacher teaches a unit and thinks about what works and what doesn't. In other words, units and assessments are always works in progress that come alive only when they are mediated by students' interests, backgrounds, and questions. This does not mean that teachers can never claim to have a solid collection of units. Teachers can evolve as designers and reach a point at which they have several units that address all or most required student outcomes and standards. The units themselves undergo some kind of transformation when they come in contact with a group of students. This transformation may be minor, as in extending or rearranging some lessons; or it may be major, as in preserving the organizing center and the culminating assessment, but replacing much of the unit content with more relevant or updated information.

Individual teachers or teams of teachers can build a successful unit by following the nine steps described below. In addition, see Appendix A for a Curriculum Unit Design Module, a Template for a Unit Sketch, and a Rubric for Developing a Curriculum Unit. The Curriculum Unit Design Module is a step-by-step list of questions and prompts that guide teachers through the development of a standards-based unit from beginning to end. The Template for a Unit Sketch enables teachers to post or list their ideas for unit lessons and assess-

> **FIGURE 3.1**
> **A TEACHER'S REPRESENTATION OF A SOCIAL STUDIES CURRICULUM**
>
> ### Units
>
> *Early man: Beginning of civilization*
> **Essential question:** What made civilization possible?
> **Concepts:** civilization, tribes, agriculture, specialization, cultural manifestations
>
> *Mesopotamia/Industrial Valley*
> **Guiding questions:** What was the most important invention to mankind? Why was the Fertile Crescent a perfect place for civilization to emerge?
> **Concepts:** civilization, culture, agriculture, specialization, human/environment interaction
>
> *Egypt*
> **Essential question:** Does Egypt qualify as a great civilization?
> **Concepts:** gods, religion, subjugation and slavery, architecture
> **Technology and mathematics application:** exploration of pyramids' structures
> **Literature connection:** The Egyptian Game
>
> *Greece*
> **Guiding question:** Is Greece the foundation of modern civilization?
> **Concepts:** sound body and mind, family, tradition, education, food, dance, city-state, culture, gods
> **Design and art connections:** comparisons with architecture in the United States modeled after Greece
> **Physical education connection:** re-enactment of first Olympics
> **Literature connection:** plays with myths and gods
>
> *Rome*
> **Essential question:** Can a civilization last forever?
> **Guiding questions:** What events can lead to the fall of an empire? What is the role of citizens in keeping a civilization strong? Is it necessary to go to war to preserve an empire? What are the similarities between Roman civilization and contemporary United States? Does everyone deserve a voice in government?
> **Concepts:** empire, citizenship, war, cultural similarities and differences, laziness, corruption, architecture
> **Design and art connections:** comparisons with architecture in the United States modeled from Rome
>
> *Middle Ages*
> **Essential question:** Mundane or magnificent?
> **Guiding question:** How were the Crusades both a success and a failure?
> **Concepts:** education, ignorance, knowledge, feudal system, literacy
> **Math connections:** impact of printing press over 500 years; comparative charts with printing numbers today
>
> *Renaissance*
> **Essential question:** Is it better to be an expert at one thing or good at many?
> **Concepts:** expertise, well-roundedness, communication, interaction, dissemination, culture
> **Science connections:** comparison of Da Vinci's diagrams of machines, human anatomy, and astrology with today's scientific models
>
> *(continues on next page)*

[
FIGURE 3.1
A TEACHER'S REPRESENTATION OF A SOCIAL STUDIES CURRICULUM *(continued)*

Contemporary Europe
Guiding question: What were the major events that changed Europe in the past 300 years?
Concepts: nationalism, citizenship, forms of government, war and peace, alliance, treaty, appeasement
Science and technology connections: advances in science technology resulting from war
Literature connections: *Diary of Anne Frank*

Vietnam
Essential question: Was the Vietnam War an exercise in futility?
Concepts: political movements, role of government, war, hero, activism
Science and technology connections: advances in science and technology resulting from war
Math connections: comparative graphs of human and other costs in Korea, World War II, and Vietnam

Exit Outcomes

Students will—
1. Recognize multiple sides or perspectives regarding issues

2. Adopt a position and support it with data
3. Identify characteristics of good citizenship
4. Appreciate cultural diversity
5. Understand the contributions of early civilizations to contemporary cultures
6. Identify the origins of contemporary United States culture
7. Identify the consequences of war
8. Work effectively in groups

Thoughts on Unit Representation

• Identification of redundancies:
Citizenship, forms of government, and war show up in many different units. I could shift some of these from one unit to another to increase the depth of treatment.

• Reconceptualization of units from themes to concepts:
I could develop one or more units centered on the three most frequently taught concepts. Perhaps I should start the year with citizenship and end with war, leaving remaining units more or less intact.

Source: Rick Hinrichs, Mattituck School District, Long Island, New York.

ments within a unit without having to elaborate on them. If teachers sketch using Post-it notes, they can easily reorganize or change the sequence of activities within a unit without investing a significant amount of time. The rubric and accompanying unit rating sheet enable teachers to self-assess their unit development work and to improve unit components that receive low ratings.

Appendix A was developed to help teachers assess and revise their curriculum units. The rubrics are not meant to be used as a summative sheet where you might add the scores to generate a grade. Instead, the rubrics should be used as formative tools whereby every rubric dimension is independent from one another. Teachers can assess their work on one or more dimensions if they want

FIGURE 3.2
CURRICULUM AND ASSESSMENT DESIGN PROCESS

Outcomes/Standards
- What do I want my students to know, be able to do and value?
- What does my district, the state or the nation want my students to know, be able to do and value?

ORGANIZING CENTER

Indicators
- What does each outcome/standard look like?
- What do they mean in my classroom/subject/grade?
- What will students produce if they are working to attain the outcomes/standards?

Learning Opportunities
- What do I need to teach or have students experience so that they will attain the learning outcomes/standards?
- What concepts/skills/processes should the unit support?

Essential and Guiding Questions
- What compelling questions could I pose to my students to focus my teaching and drive their inquiry and learning?
- What guiding questions can I use to provide coherence between different sets of lessons and activities?

Assessment
- What do I need to collect or administer to prove that students have grown toward and/or achieved desired outcomes/standards?

Performance Criteria/Rubrics
- How will I communicate what mastery or accomplishment means?
- What does quality mean for me and my students?
- How good is good enough?

Source: A preliminary version of this figure appeared in Martin-Kniep, Cunningham, & Feige (1998). Copyright © 1998 by Giselle O. Martin-Kniep. Used with permission.

to. The n/s means non-scorable. This code indicates that the teacher/author has not included sufficient information on a specific dimension for it to be scored.

1. Select an Organizing Center

As stated in Chapter 2, the organizing center is the hub of the unit—what holds it together. The many kinds of organizing centers include topics (the American Revolution, African Americans), themes (bears, aviation), concepts (war, change, flight), problems (deforestation in Brazil, violence in schools), and issues (human rights, immigration into the United States). One of the most important considerations in selecting an organizing center is the extent to which it can enable teachers to address multiple outcomes and standards.

2. State the Rationale

The rationale is the justification for a unit. It addresses the specific and important knowledge, skills, and dispositions that the unit will address, and often it incorporates the teacher's exit outcomes as well as any relevant district, state, or national standards. Following is an excerpt from a rationale for a middle school unit on conflict developed by Kim McLaughlin, Heather Bacon, and Beth Mastro with the New York State Comprehensive School Health and Wellness Program. This rationale uses current social problems and research to advocate for the unit.

> The percentage of youths aged 12–19 in 1998 who reported being victims of student violence on school grounds has risen from 3.4 percent to 4.2 percent . . . which is equal to almost one million of the twenty-four million students of that age. More than 6,000 students were expelled in 1996–1997 for bringing firearms to schools. The development of interpersonal communication

skills has demonstrated effectiveness in improving students' abilities to peaceably negotiate confrontation and reduce violence. This unit is designed with activities based on research and evaluation studies which provide evidence that the strategies used can prevent or reduce violence or disruptive behavior among youth.

The next example illustrates a different kind of rationale. Unlike the previous one, which uses statistical data on youth violence as the basis for a unit on peer mediation and peace keeping, this unit emphasizes the importance of considering humans' relationship to their environment as the basis for a unit on animal habitats and their relationship to diverse ecosystems. It is an excerpt from a rationale for a unit on the interactions between animals and their environment, developed by 5th grade teacher Lou Parrinello of the Copiague School District in Long Island, New York:

> Modern scientists utilize multiple lenses when examining a particular organism. Simply listing an animal's weight, size, and appearance is not enough to comprehend how an animal exists in relation to its environment and humankind. Zoologists and environmentalists alike study an animal's daily habitats and how it relates to the surrounding ecosystems, typically encompassing interrelationships between the animal and humans.
>
> Humanity's ever increasing impact on the surrounding environment is alarmingly apparent when looking at the changes and global effects on animals. This unit employs a student-selected animal as a vehicle to help students discover diversity within the environment, as well as relationships within the ecosystem. In addition, the examination of a particular organism is a wonderful opportunity for students to learn abstract concepts in real world situations. . . . Students will be challenged, using a series of ques-

tions and activities, to organize and synthesize information about their selected animal while drawing conclusions and identifying relationships between interdependent species.

3. Describe the Context and Present an Overview

The description of the context provides needed information about the target audience and grade level for the unit. It also describes prerequisite knowledge and skills as well as necessary time and resources for teaching the unit. The following is an excerpt from the context statement developed by Karen Ann Paquet—a former teacher in the Middle Country School District in Long Island, New York—for a 2nd grade unit that uses bread as a theme for the study of cultures:

> This unit is used as an introduction to cultures and traditional celebrations, especially during the months of October through December when holidays are numerous among people of several different cultures. It is used as a springboard for a yearlong study of different cultural groups, whether domestic or foreign.
>
> About an hour-and-a-half is needed each day to work on the unit activities and assessments, although not necessarily in one block of time. . . . The state standards integrated in this unit include languages other than English, English language arts, and social studies. While these are the only assessed standards in the unit, there are many opportunities to integrate the curriculum areas of mathematics, health, and agricultural/economic issues within the theme of bread.

Context statements need not be elaborate. The following is a context statement for the unit developed by Lou Parrinello on animals and their interactions with the environment:

> This unit was designed for a heterogeneous 5th grade classroom containing special education students and students classified as ESL (English as a second language) in a multicultural school district. The time frame involved in this unit is four weeks, with approximately 1.5 hours of daily instruction. It integrates learning standards for mathematics, science, and technology; English language arts; and social studies.

The overview of the unit's scope and activities may be linked to the context or rationale or presented as a separate, self-contained section. The following is Lou Parrinello's unit overview:

> This unit begins by having students investigate the interrelationships between animals and their environment through literature and multimedia resources. Students are guided in their learning through the use of extensive questions which are linked to their learning opportunities. . . . The culminating unit project includes an interactive multimedia and oral presentation in the form of a lesson that students have to teach to a different class.

4. Devise Essential and Guiding Questions

As described in Chapter 1, essential questions can become the centerpiece of an inquiry-driven unit. They hook students and serve as the means through which the entire unit becomes a coherent whole. Guiding questions support the essential question by framing the various sets of lessons that make up the unit. Here is an example of an essential question with supporting guiding questions for the conflict unit mentioned earlier:

> *Essential question:* When is it better not to mediate a conflict?
> *Guiding questions:* What is conflict? How is conflict different from violence? What are the roles and responsibilities of a mediator?

5. Determine Exit Outcomes and Indicators

Exit outcomes are statements that define what students will know, be able to do, and value as a result of a course of study. Here are two examples: "Students will write for a variety of purposes and audiences," and "Students will use mathematical skills and concepts to solve real-life problems." Outcomes are fairly general. They often transcend subjects and grade levels.

Outcome indicators refer to the grade-level or subject-centered characteristics of an outcome. The following are two possible indicators for the first outcome: "Students will write friendly letters," and "Students will write to convey their feelings and emotions." Outcomes and indicators are critical to the process of developing a unit because they force teachers to think about their overall picture for curriculum rather than focus on specific activities or textbook chapters. It is important for teachers to generate their own exit outcomes before identifying pertinent district, state, or national standards because it is entirely possible that they will identify an exit outcome that is important (e.g., that students are empathetic) but that has not been identified as a standard. If teachers do not consider their own exit outcomes before referring to district, state, or national standards, they might not consider incorporating their own outcomes into the curriculum and assessment design process.

6. Review District, State, and National Standards

Learning standards are becoming an increasingly prevalent component of the discourse at the district, state, and national levels. They are important to the curriculum and assessment design process because they represent a collective articulation of the needed knowledge, skills, and attitudes students should possess at different stages of their education. Unfortunately, most districts and states have developed standards independently from one another, thereby creating overlapping layers of standards that can easily become overwhelming to teachers. Some strategies for dealing with this problem include the following:

1. *Physically reconciling district, state, and national standards to incorporate their essence.* This effort can be tedious but will certainly result in more complete understanding and effective incorporation of the different kinds and levels of standards. The undertaking probably needs to be guided by a school district as a special project.

2. *Deciding on one set of standards and using it exclusively.* This can be done when a school district has adopted a specific set of standards.

3. *Adopting reconciled versions of standards.* A number of authors and organizations have done this (e.g., Kendall & Marzano, 1996).

Regardless of the strategy used, teachers should pair content with process standards so that their unit meets as many standards as possible. For example, the process standard "Students will access, generate, process, and transfer information using appropriate technologies" can be combined with the content standard "Students will use mathematical analysis, scientific inquiry, and engineering design, as appropriate, to pose questions, seek answers, and develop solutions." Teachers should also use the standards for defining performance criteria for the assessments they will administer to measure students' learning throughout the unit. For example, the standard indicator "Students will use statistical methods such as graphs, tables, and charts to interpret data" should be incorporated into the scoring rubric for an assessment in which students have to use statistics for data analysis. See Chapter

5 for a more detailed description of how teachers can develop rubrics from standards.

7. Devise Learning Opportunities

Learning opportunities are the experiences, lessons, and activities that teachers provide for students to attain targeted unit outcomes and standards. Following are several examples of learning opportunities developed by Kathy Davis—a kindergarten teacher in the Bay District Schools, Panama City, Florida—for a unit on community:

- Ask students to respond to these prompts: What do you know about your town? What makes a community? Interview students to record exact statements.
- Have children bring photos of their homes. Have each child draw a picture on 3-inch-square paper and post on a wall graph. Discuss. How are homes alike/ different?
- Have children design a chalk, oil pastel, or tempera painting of their house, using photo to guide them. Concentrate on accurate representation.
- Have children use KidPix Studio to create a computer-generated graphic representation of their home and write one sentence to describe it.

8. Develop Assessment Opportunities

Assessment opportunities include all efforts to document students' learning before (diagnostic), during (formative), and at the end of a unit segment or at the culmination of the unit (summative). To serve both teachers and students well, assessments should be seamlessly woven into the unit so that teachers can use them to support as well as measure students' learning. Following are some of the assessments that Kathy Davis uses in her unit on community:

- Pre- and post-journal questions on these prompts: What do you know about your town? What makes a community? (diagnostic and summative)
- Computer-generated representation of student's house (formative)
- Interview of student's recall of safety rules (formative)
- Interview of student's recall of the meaning of different traffic signs (formative)
- Student-generated map showing location of home relative to school and other buildings (formative)
- Observation of dramatic play focused on how to seek help in threatening situations (formative)
- Checklist of student's identification of different kinds of transportation (formative)
- Videotape and rubric of students describing their model community (summative)

The unit should include an opportunity for students to demonstrate before an audience everything they have learned in the unit by applying it in the context of dealing with a real or plausible problem. These "authentic assessments" are described at length in Chapter 4. When such assessments are used for summative purposes—that is, to give students credit or grades—they should be accompanied by explicit performance criteria in the form of checklists or rubrics. The criteria should be based on and informed by the district, state, and national standards teachers have identified. Figure 3.3 on page 23 shows the rubric that Kathy Davis uses to help her kindergarten students develop and describe a model community. She discusses each of the elements of the rubric with the children whenever she introduces another step of the work—an effective way to begin using rubrics with nonreaders. (See Chapter 5 for a complete discussion of rubrics.)

FIGURE 3.3
SCORING RUBRIC FOR A KINDERGARTEN UNIT ON COMMUNITY

	My Writing	My Community	My Building	Speaking and Listening
3	I have shown a clear awareness of the topic. I have used complete sentences and expressed myself clearly. My handwriting is legible when writing over. My illustrations are clearly recognizable and match my written words. I use lots of detail.	I know what makes up different communities. I can identify and justify the most important people, places, and things in a community. I can describe what a community would be like without these people, places, and things.	I give excellent reasons to tell why my building is important to the community. I can identify the community helpers who work in this building. I know what tools and/or vehicles are needed to do their jobs. I can describe all of the shapes associated with my building.	I look at the audience when I am talking. I speak clearly, and everyone can hear me. I stand straight and use appropriate body language. When others are speaking, I listen totally with my eyes, ears, and body.
2	I have an awareness of the topic. I have used complete sentences but may not express myself clearly. I can form most of my letters correctly when writing over. My illustrations are recognizable and match my written words but need more detail.	I know what makes up a community. I can identify some of the important people, places, and things in a community. I may not be able to describe what a community would be like without these people, places, and things.	I can tell why my building is important to the community. I may not be able to identify the helpers who work in this building, or I may not know what vehicles or tools are needed to do the jobs. I can describe the basic shape of my building.	I look only in one direction when I am speaking or sometimes look away. I may speak too softly or too loudly. When others are speaking I may not listen totally with all body parts: eyes, ears, and body. I may be moving around.
1	I may not use complete sentences, or I may not be able to express myself clearly. I can form most of my letters correctly when writing over. It is hard to tell exactly what my illustration shows. My words lack details.	I am not sure what makes up a community. I can identify only one important person, place, or thing in a community. I cannot describe what a community would be like without this person, place, or thing.	I may be confused about the name of my building, or I am not sure why my building is important to the community. I cannot correctly identify the community helpers who work in this building. I do not know the tools or vehicles needed to do their jobs. I am confused about my building's shape.	I cannot be heard clearly. I am unsure of myself, or I act very shy. I turn away from the audience.

Source: Developed by Katharine Davis. This rubric previously appeared in Center for the Study of Expertise in Teaching and Learning (CSETL). (1998). Standards-Based Curriculum and Assessment Prototypes, Vol. 4. New York: Author. Copyright © 1998 by CSETL. Reprinted by permission.

9. Develop Reflective Prompts

Reflective prompts are open-ended questions or prompts that help students think about or process their learning. They should occur throughout the unit so that teachers can monitor students' thinking and identify potential areas of confusion, misinformation, or exploration. Lou Parrinello includes the following reflective prompts in his unit on animals and their environment:

> • What did I enjoy learning most this week? Why?
> • How did it feel to have more or less than others during the role play?
> • How will what I have learned about pollution change the way I act?
> • What would I want others to do if I were an endangered species?
> • What have I learned about taking care of the earth?
> • What have I learned about a food web? How important is what I have learned?
> • What have I learned from teaching my lesson to other students? What would I do differently if I taught my lesson again?

Chapter 7 includes a comprehensive discussion of reflection.

What Do Standards-Based Units Look Like?

Most standards-based units are integrated—a characteristic that makes them easier to develop at the elementary and middle school levels. Integrating content from various subject areas is desirable because many standards can then be incorporated in a few units. Here are a few sample units:

• In a 2nd grade six-week unit titled "Technology in Our Lives," students use the scientific process and the language arts to inquire into the nature of technology. They explore simple machines, invent a technology-based gadget to solve a problem in their classroom, and design a marketing strategy for their invention. The essential question that drives this unit is, Can technology help us and hurt us at the same time?

• The 6th grade unit "Childhood" focuses on the concept of childhood and on the essential question, Are all "children" children? This is a nine-week language arts and social studies unit in which students conduct research on different countries, investigating and writing about the contexts and conditions under which children live. Following their research, students participate in panels discussing their findings and proposing solutions to childhood issues through a public showcase.

• The high school Spanish IV unit on the concept of poverty includes a literary exploration of the concept of poverty; student-driven research on poverty in different Spanish-speaking countries and among different groups in the United States; point-of-view writing about how different characters deal with poverty and survival; a discussion of two essential questions, What does it mean to be poor? and What separates survival from living?; and a panel discussion on poverty and on ways to alleviate the conditions of the poor in the local community.

Chapter 4 expands on one important aspect of unit design—namely, the development of a culminating authentic assessment that can help students use and apply everything they have learned as a result of a specific unit.

Recommended Resources

Case, R., Daniels, L., & Schwartz, P. (1996). *Critical challenges in social studies for junior high students.* Vancouver, British Columbia, Canada: The Critical Thinking Cooperative.

This book is part of a series devoted to strategies for developing students' critical thinking. The book includes 18 self-contained learning experiences addressing topics such as Buddhism, intellectual ideas of the Middle Ages, early Renaissance art, Christopher Columbus, Oliver Cromwell, and the American Revolution. Even though the series is Canadian and therefore aligned with curriculum requirements in British Columbia, the lessons are exemplary and can easily be adapted for schools in the United States.

Martin-Kniep, G. O. (1998). *Why am I doing this? Purposeful teaching with portfolio assessment.* Portsmouth, NH: Heinemann.
This book is about changing teachers' practices through extensive professional development opportunities. It is about the work of more than one hundred teachers in an initiative called the Hudson Valley Portfolio Assessment Project. It is divided into three sections. The first section explains the Hudson Valley Portfolio Assessment Project, the program components, and the design process used to develop new forms of assessment. The second section reveals several teachers' stories related to changing how they think about learning and curriculum. For example, in Chapter 5, the teacher author gives a detailed description of how she enabled her students to be responsible enough to take ownership and control of their learning. The teachers' insights are a valuable resource for teachers, administrators, and staff developers in the area of alternative assessments, portfolio development, and effective teaching. In the third part of the book, the author discusses the nature of teacher change. An appendix contains charts, teacher evaluation rubrics, and a simulation on managing change amid multiple interests.

Marzano, R. (1992). *A different kind of classroom: Teaching with Dimensions of Learning.* Alexandria, VA: Association for Supervision and Curriculum Development.
This work explores the theory and research behind the Dimensions of Learning framework and provides specific examples of the framework in action. The Dimensions framework purports to be a means for classroom restructuring that is learner-centered and is aligned with state standards. This book clarifies the framework and seeks to support schools that are using it as the basis for their school reform plans. It provides information on additional support materials such as teachers

manuals, trainer handbooks, inservice videos, and courses.

Miller, B., & Singleton, L. (1995). *Preparing citizens: Linking authentic assessment and instruction in civic/law-related education.* Boulder, CO: Social Science Education Consortium.
The target audience for this book is middle and high school social studies teachers. The book makes critical connections between civic education curriculum, instruction, and assessment. It includes a collection of authentic tasks supported by assessment procedures and emphasizes the use of rubrics in classroom instruction, including clear step-by-step instructions for development and revision. Grounded samples, methods, and suggestions for classroom instruction are presented through personal experience case studies of teachers who have used them. The teacher reflections and revisions are especially helpful in gaining better insight into designing future tasks.

Newmann, F. W., & Associates. (1996). *Authentic achievement: Restructuring schools for intellectual quality.* San Francisco, CA: Jossey-Bass.
This book presents the findings of a five-year study that researched the connection between school restructuring and student achievement. The book includes a clear discussion of the differences in cultures of schools whose restructuring efforts focus on structure, routines, and procedures versus those that attend to intellectual quality by a focus on standards. This book should be required reading for any school contemplating restructuring. It asserts that deep, meaningful change occurs when a school adopts "a sustained focus on intellectual quality (legitimacy of content, accuracy, and authenticity) and a strong professional community among staff." Too many individuals interpret restructuring as reorganizing only time and resources, focusing less on changing standards and culture. This work provides vital insight into what is needed for schools to change in substantive ways.

Wiggins, G., & McTighe, J. (1998). *Understanding by design.* Alexandria, VA: Association for Supervision and Curriculum Development.
The authors propose a "backward design" model; after determining what it is that students need to know and be able to do, assessments are designed that show evidence of this understanding. Readers are taken through this design process and provided with classroom examples as well as design templates.

Authentic Assessment

[**Essential Question:**
Can Learning in School
Be Authentic?

Educators and researchers have been advocating authentic assessments since the mid-1980s as a means to help students engage with real or plausible problems and challenges. Yet most school programs are not conducive to authentic learning experiences. In fact, one could argue that schools themselves, especially high schools, are designed to minimize authenticity. After all, how many of us experience life in 38- to 42-minute segments? This chapter defines the attributes of authentic assessment, explains how existing assessments can be refined to make them more "authentic," and demonstrates how to construct culminating authentic assessments. It provides examples of authentic assessments and guidelines for when and how to design them in different contexts.

What Is Authentic Assessment?

An assessment is authentic when it requires that students engage with real-life problems, issues, or tasks for an audience who cares about or has a stake in what students learn. Authentic tasks enable students to make sense of and apply what they have learned and to establish clear connections between what they have learned in schools and the world in which they live. Such tasks provide a wonderful opportunity for students to demonstrate what they have learned in the course of a unit and are often used as culminating projects. The following tasks are authentic:

• Following a strong storm in the area, a group of 4th grade students go to the beach to observe the problems associated with beach erosion. They read fiction and nonfiction works related to coastal environments. They then develop a series of picture books for 1st and 2nd graders on the problems associated with beach erosion and on the actions the community can take to prevent them.

• Students use imaging technology to create an autobiographical visual collage that incorporates images from a variety of sources (original photos of family and school life; original art work; magazines of interest; Internet sites; and scanned objects). They write a statement and elaborate on how or why the images depict who they are. They compare their written statement and visuals when they present and describe their collage.

• After surveying the local community to find out about the availability of summer jobs and internships, students meet with an officer from a local employment office and complete job applications for summer jobs, which they subsequently mail to prospective employers.

• To demonstrate their understanding of the geography of Egypt and of the reasons why the Nile River was essential to the ancient Egyptians, students create a game to be played by children ages 8 to 14 and market it to students in the middle school.

• Students identify and conduct research on selected environmental issues that can be addressed at the local level. They conduct extensive research on the availability of existing children's literature on those issues. They meet with a children's book publisher to discuss the specific publication demands for producing and marketing children's literature. They write a children's book on their environmental issue and test-market it in school. They

revise their book based on their test marketing and then submit it to a children's book publisher.

• Students use appropriate technology to design a phone chain that will contact their classmates in case of an emergency (assume a class of 30). They determine how long it will take to call everyone on the chain if they use a three-, four-, or five-person chain, explaining the method used to make that determination. They consider the advantages and disadvantages of using certain number chains and explain their reasoning. They present their solution to the class using a persuasive argument. The class selects the best proposal and submits it to the school office.

• Students watch and discuss a film on the Holocaust. They read *Night* by Elie Wiesel and write a personal response to the author. They then engage in a classroom discussion on human behavior and on the tendencies that supported fascism and Nazism. Students read *The Wave* by Todd Strasser or examine current data on extremist groups. They write an editorial on the extent to which the rights of such groups should be protected. Finally, among the class, they select two or three of the best editorials and submit them to the local newspaper.

• Students create a game to be played by people age 10 and older. The game will be marketed for an international corporation (predominantly French, English, and Spanish). The game has as its theme literary and historical figures who cross national boundaries. It is produced with the assistance of computer technology. Students create a game description, rules, and advertising strategies in both English and another language. They keep a journal of their progress, successes, failures, and reflections. They review copyright laws that apply to their game. They manufacture the game and offer it for sale to the student body. They select a charity that will receive the profits from the sale of the game. Finally, they communicate with businesses who might be interested in their product.

What Are the Attributes of Authenticity?

Authentic assessment tasks possess all or most of the following distinct attributes. Many of these attributes would enhance any assessment task, authentic or not.

- *Real purpose and audience.* Students solve a real problem for an invested audience beyond the classroom in a way that enables students to experience the benefits and consequences of their work.
- *Integration of content and skills.* Students build upon prior knowledge and apply knowledge and skills from two or more naturally related areas.
- *Disciplined inquiry/academic rigor.* Students search for in-depth understanding through systematic research and inquiry using a variety of primary and secondary sources.
- *Explicit standards and scoring criteria.* Students participate in the identification of performance standards for the task and in its articulation in the form of rubrics that effectively distinguish the levels of performance; performance criteria guide students in evaluation and goal setting, and a variety of exemplars and anchors illustrate various levels of performance.
- *Elaborate communication.* Students communicate what they know and can do and how they think through written, artistic, and oral performances and exhibitions, and through opportunities to teach others.

- *Levels of thinking.* Students use basic and higher levels of thinking in a task that calls for a combination of skills and forms of knowledge.
- *Reflection, self- and peer-assessment and feedback.* Students reflect on both products and processes through ongoing and specific questions, checklists, or rubrics. They formally evaluate their own and each other's learning through ongoing, elaborate, and specific feedback from both the teacher and their peers. This feedback encourages student revision to produce quality work.
- *Flexibility in content, strategies, products, and time.* The assessment task allows for student-generated choice of content and strategies; time allotment is flexible for different students and accommodates differences among the products or performances selected.

Teachers can refine existing assessment tasks to incorporate these attributes. Figure 4.1 on page 29 shows an original assessment task that a physical education teacher used with his students. Although the task—the development of a personal resistance training program—is authentic in the sense that it has a real-life purpose, it is rather narrowly defined and lacks rigor and explicit performance criteria. Figure 4.2 on pages 30–31 is a revised version of the same assessment task. The revision incorporates several of the authentic assessment attributes that were lacking in the original draft.

A teacher, or a group of teachers, may produce two or three drafts before arriving at a high-quality final product. Many school districts bring groups of teachers together in the summer or during other nonteaching times to produce two or three quality assessment design modules.

Appendix B provides tools to help teachers develop or refine an authentic assessment task. The Authentic Assessment Design Module is a step-by-

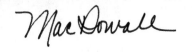

> ## FIGURE 4.1
> ## DRAFT 1 OF AN ASSESSMENT FOR A PERSONAL RESISTANCE TRAINING PROGRAM
>
> **Assessment Task:** What is the task that students will complete that will move them toward the standards and that I can collect to assess their achievement?
>
> Students will design and carry out a personal resistance training program in the school gym.
>
> **Standards:** Which standards do I teach to and assess?
>
> Health, Home Economics, and Physical Education Standard 1: Physical Education (commencement level)—Students will perform basic motor and manipulative skills . . . attain competency in a variety of physical activities . . . design personal fitness programs to improve cardiorespiratory endurance, flexibility, muscular strength, endurance, and body composition.
>
> **Indicators:** Which indicators of these standards apply to this assessment?
>
> a. Demonstrate proficiency in exercises that provide conditioning for each fitness area (muscular strength and endurance).
>
> e. Know the components of personal wellness, establish a personal profile with fitness and wellness goals, and engage in appropriate activities to improve/sustain their fitness.
>
> f. Follow a program that relates to wellness.
>
> **Teaching/Learning Opportunities:** What do I need to teach or engage students in before they work on the assessment task and while they work on the task so that they will learn and achieve the standards?
>
> Before beginning, I will teach the muscle structure, principles of training, proper techniques, and safety guidelines.
>
> While students are carrying out their training programs, I will review principles, techniques, and safety on an individual basis.
>
> **Performance Criteria:** What does a quality product or performance looks like? What are the indicators (criteria) that will form the basis of the checklist or rubric?
>
> None.
>
> *Source: Developed by Diane Cunningham. Copyright © 1998 by Learner-Centered Initiatives, Ltd. Used with permission.*

step guide through the process. The Rubric Template can be used to develop the scoring rubric that is part of the assessment. To identify the merits and shortcomings of the assessment itself, teachers can use the Rubric for Authentic Classroom Assessment Tasks and accompanying rating sheet as they design and refine.

Appendix B was developed to help teachers assess and revise their assessment tasks. The rubrics are not meant to be used as summative sheets where you might add the scores to generate a grade. Instead, the rubrics should be used as formative tools whereby every rubric dimension is independent from one another. Teachers can assess their work on one or more dimensions if they want to. The n/s means nonscorable. This code indicates that the teacher/author has not included sufficient information on a specific dimension for it to be scored.

[**FIGURE 4.2**
REVISED DRAFT OF AN ASSESSMENT FOR A PERSONAL RESISTANCE TRAINING PROGRAM

Note: The italics show what was added to the original assessment (Figure 4.1).

Assessment Task: What is the task that students will complete that will move them toward the standards and that I can collect to assess their achievement?

Students will design and carry out a personal resistance training program in the school gym *and plan a personal diet that accommodates nutritional need and activity level.*
Students will write an explanation/rationale for their design based on the principles of training.
Students will evaluate the success of their program and set goals for continuation based on principles of training and personal wellness goals.

Standards: Which standards do I teach to and measure?

Health, Home Economics, and Physical Education Standard 1: Physical Education (commencement level)—Students will perform basic motor and manipulative skills . . . attain competency in a variety of physical activities . . . design personal fitness programs to improve cardiorespiratory endurance, flexibility, muscular strength, endurance, and body composition.
Health, Home Economics and Physical Education Standard 1: Home Economics (commencement level)— Students will use an understanding of the elements of good nutrition to plan appropriate diets for themselves.
English Language Arts Standard 1: Write for information and understanding.

Indicators: Which indicators of these standards apply to this assessment?

Physical Education 1:
   a. Demonstrate proficiency in exercises that provide conditioning for each fitness area (muscular strength and endurance).
   e. Know the components of personal wellness, establish a personal profile with fitness and wellness goals, and engage in appropriate activities to improve/sustain their fitness.
   f. Follow a program that relates to wellness.

Home Economics 1:
   1a. Apply knowledge of food choices to plan a nutritional diet.
   1b. Adjust a diet to accommodate changing levels of activity and to meet nutritional needs.
   1d. Take reasoned action toward reaching personal health goals.

English Language Arts:
   2a. Write thesis/support papers on a variety of subjects.
   2d. Support decisions about training program with explicit statements and appropriate arguments.
   2f. Use standard English skillfully.

Teaching/Learning Opportunities: What do I need to teach or engage students in before they work on the assessment task and while they work on the task so that they will learn and achieve the standards?

Before beginning, I will teach the muscle structure, principles of training, proper techniques, and safety guidelines.
Before beginning, students will be required to read an informational packet on nutrition to review the elements of good nutrition.
Before beginning, I will show several models of effective training programs and describe the qualities of an effective training program (using a checklist or rubric).
Students will pair up and assess each other's plans using the checklist provided.
While students are carrying out their training programs, I will review principles, techniques, and safety on an individual basis *and use the checklist to assess students.*

(continues on next page)

> ## FIGURE 4.2
> ## REVISED DRAFT OF AN ASSESSMENT FOR A PERSONAL RESISTANCE TRAINING PROGRAM *(continued)*
>
> **Performance Criteria:** What does a quality product or performance look like? What are the indicators (criteria) that will form the basis of the checklist or rubric?
>
> *Checklist for Personal Training Program Plan*
> ☐ *Student's fitness goals are clearly identified.*
> ☐ *Accurate and appropriate weight/starting point for each exercise.*
> ☐ *Program follows the rule of specificity.*
> ☐ *Program follows the rule of progression.*
> ☐ *Program follows the rule of overload—frequency, intensity, time.*
> ☐ *Rationale for plan is clearly explained.*
> ☐ *The rationale identifies the training principles that are applied and explains why actions are included in relation to the student's personal goals.*
>
> *Checklist for Implementation of Training Program*
> ☐ *Workouts are recorded each day on the daily log.*
> ☐ *Adjustments are made when necessary.*
> ☐ *Adjustments are appropriate considering the student's individual fitness goals.*
> ☐ *Proper technique is used at each station.*
> ☐ *Safety precautions (____, ____, ___) are followed.*
>
> *Checklist for Evaluation and Goal Setting*
> ☐ *Student discusses what worked well and why.*
> ☐ *Student describes adjustments made, why they were made, and what effect they had.*
> ☐ *Student describes what didn't work and why.*
> ☐ *Student describes possible next steps in relation to the continuation of the personal training program, personal fitness goals, and the fitness principles of specificity, progression, and overload.*
>
> *Checklist for Personal Diet*
> ☐ *Student's fitness and nutrition goals are clearly identified.*
> ☐ *Diet is balanced, drawing from all food groups.*
> ☐ *Diet accommodates additional activity of resistance training.*
> ☐ *Rationale for the diet is clearly explained.*
> ☐ *The rationale identifies the nutritional elements that are present and explains why they are included in relation to the student's personal goals and training program.*
> ☐ *Diet log includes meals for each day.*
>
> *Source: Developed by Diane Cunningham. Copyright © 1998 by Learner-Centered Initiatives, Ltd. Used with permission.*

Recommended Resources

Burke, K. (Ed.). (1996). *Authentic assessment: A collection.* Palatine, IL: IRI/Skylight Publications.
This collection succinctly dispels the myth that authentic assessment is a contemporary "buzz word." Through a collection of writings, this text traces the history of trends in the National Assessment of Educational Progress (NAEP), competency testing, and the influences of the National Governors Association upon authentic instruction. It then defines, explains, and provides exemplars of authentic, alternative assessments. Many secondary examples are included. In addition, each section includes an extensive bibliography of related articles. Its readability and compilation of exemplars make this a valuable text for anyone wanting to develop their assessment literacy.

Hart, D. (1994). *Authentic assessment: A handbook for educators.* New York: Addison-Wesley.
This book is an excellent primer about assessment. It provides readers with a basic understanding and knowledge of assessment and related issues. Each chapter contains definitions of pertinent terms and provides many examples in chart or graph form. The book also includes an extensive glossary of assessment terms and a bibliography of supporting resources in assessment. The topics covered by this book include standardized testing vis-à-vis authentic assessment; portfolio assessment; performance assessment; and scoring and grading strategies.

Hill, C., & Norwick, L. (1998). *Classroom-based assessment.* Norwood, MA: Christopher-Gordon Publishing.

This book is the first of four in a series on assessment. It presents practical ways to collect information about young learners. It addresses teacher notebooks and observing as assessment continuums, and includes assessment forms and recommended readings. The text is easy to understand, and the sample forms are valuable. Although the emphasis is on assessments in reading and writing, other content areas are also covered.

Johnson, B. (1996). *Performance assessment handbook, volume 2.* Princeton, NJ: Eye on Education.
The author begins by discussing the evolution of assessment during the 20th century. He describes a flawed product based on fragmented curriculum designed for cellular classrooms that processed students, moving them on or dropping them out. The book builds a case against traditional testing methods and advocates for the use of performances and exhibitions to assess student learning.

Kuhn, T. (1992). *Mathematics assessment: Alternative approaches* [Videotape]. Columbia, SC: National Council of Teachers of Mathematics.
This video and viewer guide focuses on alternative assessment in mathematics. The video is divided into six segments that cover the introduction and implementation of alternative assessment in the mathematics classroom. Each video segment has two parts: classroom and faculty interactions and panel discussions. The guide provides summaries of the videos and extended activities for staff development. This is a good tool for staff developers to use to introduce alternative assessment in mathematics.

McCollum, S. L. (1994). *Performance assessment in the social studies classroom: A how-to book for teachers.* Joplin, MO: Chalk Dust Press.
This book explores authentic social studies performance assessments in grades 4–12. Each of the 14 individual tasks is directly tied to social studies concepts, content, and skills, and related to real-world experiences. The author (a social studies teacher) gives the reader clearly outlined task instructions, materials, blackline masters, task-specific rubrics, student checklists, and examples of students' work. McCollum tries to design a formula for success by providing clear and precise guidelines for designing performance assessment tasks.

Miller, B., & Singleton, L. (1995). *Preparing citizens: Linking authentic assessment and instruction in civic/law-related education.* Boulder, CO: Social Science Education Consortium.
This book makes critical connections among civic education curriculum, instruction, and assessment. It presents a collection of authentic tasks supported by assessment procedures. The strong emphasis on the use of rubrics in classroom instruction is supported by clear step-by-step instructions for developing and revising rubrics. The authors present grounded samples, methods, and suggestions for classroom instruction through personal experience/case studies of teachers who have used them. The teacher reflections and revisions are also especially helpful in providing an insight into the design of tasks.

Newman, F. W., Secada, W. G., & Wehlage, G. G. (1995). *A guide to authentic instruction and assessment: Vision, standards and scoring.* Wisconsin Center for Education Research, 1025 West Johnson Street, Room 242, Madison, WI 53706; (608) 263-4214; cost: $9.00.
This book identifies three criteria for authentic learning tasks: the construction of knowledge, disciplined inquiry, and value beyond school. The authors discuss these criteria as they relate to tasks, instruction, and student performance and further break down the three criteria into standards. They provide examples from math and social studies for each of the standards identified. These examples cross grade levels. Finally, the text provides scoring criteria for judging the authenticity of assessment tasks, instruction, and student performance.

Stiggins, R. J. (1994). *Student-centered classroom assessment.* New York: Merrill Publishing.
The book focuses on ways to develop and use sound classroom assessments and on strategies to involve students as partners in the assessment process. It presents a balanced look at all kinds of assessments. It includes a variety of classroom applications; discusses ways to communicate student achievement, including report cards versus portfolios; and provides a reflection section that could be used in staff development activities.

Strickland, J., & Strickland, K. (1998). *Reflections on assessment: Its purposes, methods and effects on learning.* Portsmouth, NH: Boynton/Cook Publishers, Inc.

This book provides a clear picture of what assessment is. It begins with definitions and a historical background section and continues with strategies for assessment and evaluation in the classroom and their political implications. Examples of assessments that are in place across the country are integrated throughout the book with explanations of how the teachers meet state mandates and the needs of their students. There are also personal essays by teachers and students about assessments that are used daily in classrooms.

Webb, N. L. (Ed.). (1993). *Assessment in the mathematics classroom.* Reston, VA: National Council of Teachers of Mathematics, Inc.

This text includes introductory chapters on the mathematics classroom and assessment in general. The body of the text is grouped into assessments by educational levels: K–4, 5–8, and 9–12. The book concludes with three chapters on issues to think about in classroom assessment.

Wiggins, G. (1998). *Educative assessment: Designing assessments to inform and improve student performance.* San Francisco: Jossey-Bass.

This book is aimed at enabling educators to create assessments that will improve performance and not merely audit it. It calls for the use of authentic tasks, feedback mechanisms for teacher and students while learning is in progress, and resulting adjustments during the entire process. It is replete with charts, graphs, examples, and diagrams that make the book both readable and practical. The models provided can actually be altered and used in the classroom without much effort. Standards and criteria are explained and samples of rubrics included. The rubric construction is thoroughly demonstrated. The author also explores the intricacies of portfolio assessment and provides sample charts for inclusion and evaluation.

Using Scoring Rubrics to Support Learning

[**Essential Question:**
How Do We Communicate What
We Mean by "Good"?

R ubrics are rapidly becoming accepted in many schools and classrooms. They are a critical component of authentic assessment tasks and of other assessments used to evaluate students' learning and to assign grades. However, most people associate rubrics with explicit grading criteria, and little has been said about the role that rubrics can have in supporting, and not just measuring, learning. This chapter explores rubrics as tools for teaching and learning.

What Is a Rubric?

A rubric is a rating scale that defines and differentiates levels of performance. It is different from checklists, scoring sheets, and rating scales. Unlike checklists, rubrics do more than look for the presence or absence of an attribute. Rubrics differ from scoring sheets in that they do more than in-

dicate that a specific quality or attribute is worth a given number of points. Finally, rubrics are different from rating scales because they do more than look for degrees of completeness or emphasis. A rubric actually identifies all the needed attributes of quality or development in a process, product, or performance and defines different levels for each of these attributes.

What Are the Different Types of Rubrics?

Many kinds of rubrics appear in the education marketplace. However, most classroom rubrics are either holistic or analytic. Holistic rubrics assign a single score to an entire product, process, or performance. By design, they capture the whole of a product instead of emphasizing its parts. They rely on multiple descriptors but refer to them in single clauses or paragraphs. Because of their holistic nature, these rubrics are limited in value in terms of providing precise diagnostic information to students. This is especially true for students whose work falls in the middle levels of performance and who may have a difficult time teasing out specifically what they need to do to improve. Holistic rubrics are difficult to construct because it is challenging to clearly differentiate one level from another when all the attributes are listed together. On the other hand, these rubrics are easier to use as scoring tools than are analytic rubrics because only one score is needed. Figure 5.1 is an example of a holistic rubric.

Analytic scoring rubrics disaggregate the parts of a product, process, or performance into its critical attributes or dimensions. They describe each of

these attributes separately and have descriptors for each attribute. These rubrics make it easy for the learner to identify the specific strengths and weaknesses of a work and to know what to do to make improvements. These rubrics are easier to construct than holistic rubrics, but they take longer to score because each quality, attribute, or dimension of the work receives a different score. Figure 5.2 is a rather playful example of an analytic scoring rubric, in this case describing attributes of students.

Both holistic and analytic rubrics can vary in their degree of specificity. Figure 5.3 is an example of a generic rubric for problem solving developed by Maria Mondini, a mathematics teacher in Suffolk County, New York. It can be used by math teachers at any grade level to score all kinds of problems. With some adaptation, it can also be

---

FIGURE 5.1
A HOLISTIC RUBRIC FOR A PERSUASIVE LETTER

6   Takes a strong, convincing position; is well-organized; argument is persuasive with accurate, supporting evidence; discusses all significant issues with clear understanding of important relationships; examines the problem from several different positions using arguments and counterarguments.

5   Takes a well-defined position; organizes argument with supporting evidence from a variety of sources; discusses the major issues and shows an understanding of the relationships among them.

4   Offers a clear, plausible position; organized argument with adequate evidence from limited sources; considers several ideas or aspects of the issue.

3   Offers a specific position; presentation has logical organization; limited evidence applied to general conclusion; considers more than one idea or aspect of the issue.

2   Offers general position; presentation has minimal organization; uses generalities and personal opinion to support position; considers only one aspect of the issue.

1   Position is vague; presentation is brief with unrelated general statements; view on issue is not clear; statements tend to wander or ramble.

FIGURE 5.2
AN ANALYTIC RUBRIC FOR STUDENT ATTRIBUTES

Dimension	1	2	3	4	5	6
Preparedness	Doesn't know what a book is.	Doesn't know where the book is.	Knows where the book is but doesn't have it.	Has book, but it's the wrong book.	Has right book, but it's not open.	Has right book open to right page.
Participation	Is absent.	Is present but at the nurse's office.	Is in the right hall but in the wrong room.	Is in the right room, asleep at someone else's desk.	Is in the right room, asleep at own desk.	Is in the right desk and awake.
Hygiene	Has seen water.	Recognizes soap and water.	Uses water weekly.	Uses soap and water weekly.	Uses soap and water and knows what deodorant is.	Uses soap, water, and deodorant daily.

used to assess problem solving in any area. On the other hand, Figure 5.4 (p. 38) is an excerpt from a task-specific rubric that was designed by Pat Lynch—a teacher in the Manhasset School District in Long Island, New York—to help students become teaching volunteers at the Museum of Natural History in New York City.

The more specific a rubric is, the more helpful it is to students. Sometimes a generic rubric is too far removed from the demands of a specific project, and students cannot use it to get the information they need to guide their work.

Finally, rubrics can also be developmental—that is, they can be used to assess students along a developmental or grade-level continuum. Figure 5.5 (p. 39) is a rubric developed by a group of teachers from the Manhasset School District in Long Island, New York. They use it to assess students' develop-

ing proficiencies around one of the district's exit standards: informed opinion. The primary advantage of such a rubric is that it enables teachers in different subjects and grades to share a language and an assessment tool.

Why Use Rubrics?

Rubrics have enormous value as instructional tools and as assessment tools. They are useful to teachers because they help them clarify what they want from students and convey their expectations for students' work and achievement in ways that students can understand and use. Even if, after developing a rubric, teachers do not share it with their students, the process of developing the rubric will have a positive effect on teachers' instruction, be-

---

FIGURE 5.3
A RUBRIC FOR PROBLEM SOLVING

Dimension	4	3	2	1
Understanding of the problem	Can restate the question in own words and explain it to others using different examples.	Can restate the question in own words.	Has difficulty restating the question, but indicates some understanding of the problem.	Cannot restate or paraphrase the question. Is able only to repeat the question.
Planning	Identifies multiple strategies and selects the best strategy for solving the problem.	Identifies necessary steps to solve the problem. Is able to identify the parts of the problem.	Identifies a strategy to solve part of the problem.	Generates strategies that have nothing to do with the problem, or cannot determine which strategy to use.
Procedure	Provides a clear, step-by-step explanation of the procedure and explains why each step was taken.	Provides a clear, step-by-step explanation of the procedure.	Describes procedure in way that includes some, but not all, necessary steps for solving the problem.	Lays out problem without thought or explanation of the procedure.
Assessment	Gives correct and thorough answer(s). Clearly explains why the answer is logical and makes connections between the solution and solutions to similar problems.	Gives correct answer(s). Clearly explains why the answer is logical	Gives partially correct answer that could be arrived at logically.	Gives answer that is incorrect and is not supported by a plausible conclusion.

Source: Adapted from a rubric developed by Maria Mondini, East Hampton School District, Long Island, New York.

---

cause they will be clearer in articulating what they want.

Students benefit from rubrics because they can use them to identify the attributes of exemplary work. Rubrics assist students as they proceed with the development of processes and products helping them monitor their own performance and achievement.

Rubrics are also helpful to other stakeholders because they enable teachers to justify and validate grades, and they allow people such as parents, supervisors, and support staff to see teachers' criteria

FIGURE 5.4
A RUBRIC FOR ORAL PRESENTATION SKILLS FOR MUSEUM VOLUNTEERS

Dimension	Superior	Good	Satisfactory	Needs Improvement
Articulation	Gave a highly articulate presentation. Spoke clearly and distinctively, with careful enunciation, lively expression. Used distinctive style or manner of expression. Speaking was easily perceptible to museum visitors, and its expressive quality enhanced the power of the speaking.	Vocal expression was clear and distinct. Museum visitors could hear and understand the volunteer's spoken words.	Vocal expression was clear at times and indistinct at other times. Museum visitors occasionally had difficulty hearing and understanding the volunteer's spoken words.	Speaking was indistinct, with mumbled and/or slurred words, careless enunciation. Museum visitors were unable to understand the speaking.
Pace of Delivery	Pace was consistently appropriate for museum visitors to take in the material—neither too fast nor too slow. Adjusted pace to meet visitors' needs. Presentation was completed on time, and the pace was steady throughout.	Steady pace was neither too fast nor too slow. Some adjustments were needed to complete presentation on time. Adjustments didn't interfere with museum visitors' experience.	Pace was inconsistent—at times too fast or too slow. Museum visitors felt rushed at times or that the presentation dragged at others. Tour finished close to the allotted time.	Pace was too fast or too slow. Tour finished too early or too late.
Physical Presentation	Maintained an engaging yet calm, poised, professional demeanor at all times and under all circumstances. Maintained appropriate eye contact throughout. All gestures and motions were appropriate and enhanced the speaking and the audience's comfort level and participation. Body position didn't block visitors' view of exhibits.	Appeared comfortable in role. Postures, motions, and body language were appropriate. Body position did not block view of exhibits.	Posture, motions, and body language were distracting at times. Sometimes appeared anxious or disinterested, but comfortable at other times. Eye contact was mostly appropriate; at times volunteer avoided eye contact or stared inappropriately. Body position at times blocked museum visitors' view of exhibits.	Body language suggested anxiety or disinterest. Appeared uncomfortable with the role. Motions, gestures, and body language were distracting for museum visitors. Body position interfered with view of exhibits.

Source: Adapted from a rubric developed by P. Lynch. Copyright © 1997 by Center for the Study of Expertise in Teaching and Learning (CSETL). Used with permission.

FIGURE 5.5
A RUBRIC FOR DEVELOPING AND SUPPORTING AN INFORMED OPINION

Indicator	Not Yet Proficient	Proficient	Highly Proficient	Advanced
Selects and/or explores an area of inquiry.	Explores an area of inquiry with significant support.	Chooses an area with little direction from teacher after exploring several sources.	Chooses area with no direction from teacher after exploring a variety of types of sources.	Chooses area based upon genuine curiosity after developing a "feel" for the broader area of inquiry.
Uses an established research process to explore primary and secondary sources to garner information.	Needs interpretation of basic guidelines, and the sources must be identified for the student.	Explores sufficient sources to meet basic guidelines of the assigned research.	Explores many primary and secondary sources and prioritizes the value of all of the source of inquiry material.	Seeks primary and secondary sources of proven value by going beyond what is readily available. Seeks obscure sources to verify previous source material.
Demonstrates a working knowledge of the area of inquiry, including its specialized vocabulary and its connection to other fields of study, especially interdisciplinary patterns and concepts that aid understanding.	Has an introductory or basic knowledge of the research area.	Is conversant about major aspects of the research area.	Uses vocabulary of the field and understands how the research fits into the parameters of the overall area and other related areas.	Uses vocabulary of the "real world," is knowledgeable about the issues or problems of the field and other related areas, and predicts future developments.
Collects and synthesizes information in support of the opinion.	Is able to collect information with support.	Is able to restate the collected information in own words.	With an open mind, rethinks initial view or position by evaluating and integrating the new information.	With an open mind, rethinks initial view or position by evaluating and synthesizing the new information in a unique way that helps others understand the range of views.

(continues on next page)

FIGURE 5.5
A RUBRIC FOR DEVELOPING AND SUPPORTING AN INFORMED OPINION (*continued*)

Indicator	Not Yet Proficient	Proficient	Highly Proficient	Advanced
Interacts with others to consider a range of opinions as a basis for formulating own opinion.	Listens to others' views or opinions but is unable to paraphrase them.	Listens to and is able to paraphrase others' positions or views.	With an open mind, rethinks initial view or position by evaluating and integrating the new information.	With an open mind, rethinks initial view or position by evaluating and synthesizing the new information in a unique way that helps others understand the range of views.
Develops essential questions/problem statement/thesis statement.	Needs help developing the essential questions so that research can begin.	Develops question(s) that can be researched.	Develops essential questions that lead to a research plan and relate to the thesis.	Develops essential question(s) that strike the audience as unique and important.
Distinguishes between relevant and irrelevant, accurate and inaccurate sources.	Needs significant support to determine accuracy and relevance of the information.	Can rate all obtained information as to its accuracy and relevance to the question(s) posed.	Identifies bias in sources, looks for errors in research methods, and follows up on discrepancies.	Defends sources with evidence, cross-references, and considerable independent research.
Defends opinion in written, oral, or presentation formats using established conventions of language and with sense of audience.	Presentation is unclear, and conclusion is not supported with evidence.	Presentation is clear, and conclusion is supported by ample evidence.	Presentation can be described as novel and complete. It anticipates opposing points of view.	Presentation evokes an emotional response in the audience. Standards of presentation could be applied in real-world scenarios.
Recommends how the findings may have practical application in solving problems within given constraints and acceptable ethical limits.	Does not discover practical applications in solving problems.	Offers a solution to a previously identified problem based upon own informed opinion without identifying ramifications.	Suggests new problems or challenges but does not ground them in own research or suggest ways to develop solutions.	Suggests new problems or challenges that might result and appreciates the ways in which these new understandings have changed own views. Is able to identify possible approaches for future work.

Source: Adapted from a rubric developed by teachers in the Manhasset School District in Long Island, New York.

for judging students' work. Because they remove the mystery from the attributes of quality work, rubrics often lead to an overall increase in the quality of students' work.

When Should Rubrics Be Used? What Deserves a Rubric?

Rubrics are most useful when they depict processes, performances, and products found in the real world. Among the processes and dispositions that lend themselves to the development of rubrics are cooperative learning, discussions, critical thinking, and habits of mind. Figure 5.6 shows a rubric for cooperative learning developed by Iris Gandler, an elementary school teacher in the Manhasset School District in Long Island, New York. Figure 5.7 shows a rubric for critical thinking developed by Cindy Shepardson, an enrichment teacher in the Newark School District in Newark, New York.

Rubrics for processes are fairly generic and can be used as soon as teachers want students to learn the "rules of the game" for those processes. They can be used throughout the year in all kinds of assignments that require the same processes.

Rubrics can also support performances, including debates, role plays, artistic presentations, mock trials, and persuasive speeches. Figure 5.8 (pp. 46–47) is a rubric for a persuasive speech.

Rubrics can also be developed for authentic products—that is, products that can be illustrated by exemplars or models obtained outside of schools. Products worth developing rubrics for include research papers, museum exhibits, lab reports, investigations, stories, poems, and artistic products. Figure 5.9 (pp. 48–49) is a rubric for a laboratory report developed by Lisa Boerum, a spe-

cial education teacher in the Sag Harbor School District in Sag Harbor, New York. It encompasses elements related to both science and language arts.

Process and product rubrics can vary in specificity, depending on the situation. Often teachers find that rubrics for different processes and products can retain several of the same dimensions or attributes, and require only one or two changes. For example, in a scientific investigation, regardless of its focus, students may need to develop a problem statement, generate a hypothesis, define data collection procedures, conduct a data analysis, and generate conclusions. Some investigations may need a literature review, and others may need supporting visuals. Teachers can recycle a rubric by simply changing the language in one or more dimensions or by adding a dimension to their original version.

Finally, rubrics can be developed for units or for essential questions. Figure 5.10 (pp. 50–51) is a rubric developed in response to the question: Does Egypt qualify as a great civilization? The rubric was developed by Rick Hinrichs, a middle school teacher in Mattituck, New York. He used it for pre- and post-tests.

What Are the Components and Quality Attributes of Rubrics?

All rubrics have levels, dimensions, and descriptors. Levels indicate the range of performance measured, from least developed to most developed. Dimensions are the attributes used to judge a performance, process, or product. Descriptors refer to the language used to define the dimensions in the different levels.

Three things contribute to the quality of rubrics: (1) content, (2) structure or form, and (3) layout.

[**FIGURE 5.6**
[**A RUBRIC FOR COOPERATIVE LEARNING**

Dimension	4	3	2	1
TEAMWORK* **How well did your group work together?**	Worked extremely well together; provided a "model" to other groups; stayed "on task," involving each member and taking teamwork seriously; highly productive.	Worked very well together; were productive and cooperative; worked to get everyone involved.	Attempted to work well most of the time; "off task" at times, with all members not actively involved, thus diminishing the overall effectiveness of the group. Responsibility shared by half the group members.	Little or no teamwork involved. Did not respect one another's opinions and disagreed over group's work. Exclusive reliance on one person.
ACTIVE LEARNING **How well did your group seek solutions?**	Extremely clever in seeking different solutions through "risk taking" and exploring different approaches and strategies in an original and/or creative way.	Clever at times in seeking solutions through "risk taking" and exploring different approaches and strategies.	Attempted to seek solutions through different approaches and strategies.	Little evidence of exploring different approaches and strategies.
COMMUNICATION **How well did your group communicate and share information?**	Went above and beyond in communicating thought processes and strategies by asking questions, discussing ideas, listening, offering constructive criticism, and summarizing discoveries.	Did a very good job of communicating thought processes and strategies by asking questions, discussing ideas, and listening.	Attempted to communicate thought processes and strategies but did not listen to constructive criticism.	Group members worked individually at the table together and did not communicate with one another. Group members had trouble "listening" to one another's thoughts and ideas showing a lack of respect.

*Source: Adapted from a rubric developed by Iris Gandler. Copyright © 1997 by Center for the Study of Expertise in Teaching and Learning (CSETL). Used with permission. *Teamwork criteria from Putnam Valley Project Assessment Chart.*

FIGURE 5.7
A RUBRIC FOR PRINCIPLES OF CRITICAL THINKING

Objective: *Students will demonstrate an understanding of and the use of the major "principles" (strategies)* of critical thinking in their writing, speaking, and actions.*

	LEVELS OF PERFORMANCE			
Element	**Exemplary (3)**	**Developed (2)**	**Emerging (1)**	**Undeveloped (0)**
Intellectual Perseverance (S[Strategy]–8)	Clearly shows a willingness to go back to previous reflections to reconsider, reanalyze, and/or add to them. Confusion, unsettled questions, or ongoing and continuous struggles with complex ideas are evident.	Demonstrates, by revisiting ideas more than once, a willingness to reanalyze ideas to get to a better understanding. Reflection shows some struggle with complexity.	Has made an obvious effort to revisit previous reflections; additions, however, are superficial and relate only to simple, rather than complex, ideas.	Demonstrates no evidence of revisiting initial thoughts to reanalyze or add to them. An attitude of "just getting something down on paper" seems prevalent.
Developing One's Perspective (S–12)	Demonstrates a clear understanding of own beliefs and has indicated other ideas or possibilities that may impact that perspective. Analyzes the credibility of these thoroughly. Does not uncritically accept viewpoints of peers or society. May present changes in perspective.	Can state his or her perspective clearly and also demonstrates a conscious effort to analyze other perspectives in relation to own present belief.	Can state perspective clearly and demonstrates a conscious effort to seek and analyze additional views.	States a personal belief or perspective, somewhat vaguely, and seeks no other viewpoints. May take an egocentric or sociocentric stand (only the student's ideas are right). May adopt generally accepted views of peers or society without thought.

(continues on next page)

FIGURE 5.7
A RUBRIC FOR PRINCIPLES OF CRITICAL THINKING (continued)

LEVELS OF PERFORMANCE

Element	Exemplary (3)	Developed (2)	Emerging (1)	Undeveloped (0)
Generating and Selecting Solutions (S–19)	Studies and analyzes the causes of problem situations at length and chooses "best" solutions based on specific and highly appropriate criteria that student identifies. When solutions are not apparent, student generates them. Deliberately and consistently takes into account the interests of everyone affected by the problem and proposed solution(s).	Functions independently through all steps of generating and assessing solutions (identifying/generating solutions, determining appropriate criteria, selecting initial solutions, determining possible effects and consequences, choosing best solutions) but does so less thoroughly than might be necessary.	Easily identifies or generates and then selects solutions to problem situations when the criteria for selection are very apparent or given. When pushed, will consider possible consequences of certain solutions, but rarely does this extensively or independently.	If or when solutions to problems are not readily apparent, offers a sloppy or self-serving description of the situation and "leaps" to a quick-fix solution. Makes no effort to determine possible causes or effects of specific actions. Concentrates on getting own way (may have hidden agendas).
Analyzing and Evaluating Actions and Policies (Exploring Consequences) (S–20; S–35)	Considers and analyzes both the positive and negative aspects of the idea(s) in question. Generates a thorough list of criteria. Judgment is based on clear and specific criteria (offering a thorough look at possible effect of action on others). Appropriately justifies thinking, offering multiple reasons based on this criteria.	Thoroughly considers positive and negative consequences of actions. Independently generates a list of appropriate criteria by which to judge specific actions (at least two of which relate to the action's effect on others). Gives many varied reasons to justify actions.	Makes an effort to consider possible consequences of actions. Both positive and negative effects are evident but not extensive. Uses criteria if given, and may generate one or two independently. Gives one or two reasons for actions, and at least one of these relates directly to criteria listed.	Chooses the first thing that comes to mind and acts impulsively. No reference to criteria and/or consequences of actions made. Does not justify the actions with reasons.

FIGURE 5.7
A RUBRIC FOR PRINCIPLES OF CRITICAL THINKING *(continued)*

	LEVELS OF PERFORMANCE			
Element	Exemplary (3)	Developed (2)	Emerging (1)	Undeveloped (0)
Noting Significant Differences and Similarities (S–29)	Is highly sensitive to the existence of various similarities and differences in things and seeks to determine significance. Considers these deeply, hesitating to classify or make comparisons based on superficial information. Independently seeks to determine various classifications.	Same as "Emerging," but independently shifts categories to incorporate various significant similarities and differences. May not independently seek similarities and differences when certain categories are already in place without prompting.	Easily analyzes a number of possible similarities and differences. May not shift easily from categories once found initially, however. May need continued assistance to identify "significant" differences and likenesses that may change categories.	Fails to take the time to determine or identify significant similarities and/or differences, taking things at "face value," superficially categorizing or labeling things, people, etc., based on trivial or insignificant information. Forms stereotypes quickly.
Thinking Independently (S–1)	Diligently incorporates all known knowledge (seeks new knowledge) and insight into thoughts and behavior. Demonstrates a willingness to think things out for own self. Is not easily manipulated by others. Is *self-monitoring*, catching own errors in thinking. Can determine when information is relevant, when to apply a concept or to use a specific skill.	Seeks understanding of ideas *independently, without prompting*. Deliberately considers new perspectives and ways of doing things as a matter of course. Will risk presenting or accepting new ideas or actions when based on the contributions of genuine authorities. Thinking still requires *some monitoring*. Can detect manipulation and resists it.	Makes a conscious effort to seek an understanding of ideas before taking a stand on them, by asking questions and gathering additional information from other sources *when prompted*. Will at least consider new ways of looking at things, but often stays within already accepted ways of doing things. Can detect manipulation and resists it.	Is limited by the "accepted" way of doing things. Is hesitant to think for himself or herself; may mindlessly accept the ideas of peers or society. Waits for others to determine errors in thinking and set the course of action. May accept or reject ideas or beliefs not understood. Resists considering "new" ways of looking at things.

Source: Adapted from a rubric developed by Cindy Shepardson, Newark School District, Newark, New York. Copyright © 1997, 2000, by Cindy Shepardson. Used with permission.
*Reference: Foundation for Critical Thinking (2000, January 28). Strategy List: 35 Dimensions of Critical Thought. Retrieved from the World Wide Web (http://www.criticalthinking.org/K12/k12class/strataIl.nclk).

FIGURE 5.8
A RUBRIC FOR A PERSUASIVE SPEECH

Dimension	4	3	2	1
Success	Receives most votes.	Receives above median number of votes.	Receives below median number of votes.	Receives the least number of votes.
Audience Appeal	Demonstrates a sound understanding of the audience and adapts message to their interests and needs.	Argument appeals to the interests and needs of the audience in general.	Demonstrates limited knowledge of the audience; arguments are loosely related to the audience's needs or interests.	Demonstrates no understanding of the audience; arguments are pertinent to an audience that is not in the room.
Content	Demonstrates an in-depth understanding of the concepts; uses extensive and relevant examples, analogies/comparisons; responds confidently and accurately to questions from audience.	Demonstrates an understanding of specific concepts; uses relevant examples; responds accurately to questions from the audience.	Demonstrates a basic understanding of the concepts; uses few relevant examples; responds to questions from the audience in a limited and cursory manner.	Demonstrates an inaccurate or flawed understanding of the concepts; speaks in generalities without supporting examples; ignores the audience's questions.
Presentation	Delivers speech with clarity, enthusiasm, and flawless inflection; uses note cards only as occasional reminders or to cite a direct quotation; pace and volume allow audience to follow the entire presentation;	Delivers speech clearly, with appropriate inflection; refers to note cards regularly, interrupting the smoothness of the presentation; pace and volume make listening possible; makes eye contact with	Speech is hampered by lack of energy and enthusiasm. Presentation is primarily read. Pace is erratic and voice tends to fall at the end of sentences. Eye contact is limited to one member of the audience	Speech is inaudible. All that is presented is read. Mumbles; looks down or away from the audience; movements distract from presentation.

FIGURE 5.8
A RUBRIC FOR A PERSUASIVE SPEECH *(continued)*

Dimension	4	3	2	1
Presentation *(continued)*	constantly uses eye contact with the entire audience; gestures are purposeful and add to the presentation.	several members of the audience; gestures are somewhat contrived.	or is infrequent; gestures lack purpose and detract from presentation.	
Organization	Listeners easily follow and understand the logical and smooth arguments and their relationship to each other.	Listeners are able to understand the purpose of the speech because of the logical organization of the arguments.	Listeners are able to understand the purpose of the speech, but the loose organization makes the central argument unclear.	Listener is unable to follow the arguments being made because of their illogical arrangement.
Language usage	No errors in usage.	Errors in usage are so minor that they must be searched for.	Errors in usage interfere with listeners' understanding of the presentation.	Errors in usage are so prevalent that the audience cannot understand what is being said.

FIGURE 5.9
A RUBRIC FOR A SCIENCE LAB

Dimensions	Novice	Apprentice	Practitioner	Expert
Purpose • Problem	• A topic sentence is written, but a problem or question needs to be defined.	• A problem or question is defined, but reasons need to be made clear.	• A problem or question is defined with reasons.	• Problem to be solved or question to be answered is defined with clear, detailed reasons and examples.
• Hypothesis	• A statement is written, but it needs to be formed into a hypothesis.	• Hypothesis needs to be related to the problem or question.	• Hypothesis needs to be in the format of an educated guess.	• Hypothesis is formulated as an educated guess about the possible solution or answer.
Materials	• Materials are listed but are not appropriate for the experiment.	• Materials that are listed are appropriate, but the list is incomplete.	• Materials are listed and complete, but the amount needs to be included.	• Type and amount of materials are complete and appropriate for the experiment.
Procedure • Sequence	• Plan is written but needs to be told in a logical order.	• Plan is in sequence but needs description and explanation.	• Plan has logical sequence, with descriptions, but explanations need to clarify why steps were taken.	• Plan has logical sequence, supported by step-by-step descriptions and clear, logical explanations as to why the steps were taken.
• Appropriateness	• Plan needs to be re-designed to prove hypothesis.	• Plan indirectly relates to the hypothesis.	• Plan relates to the hypothesis.	• Plan is appropriately designed to clearly prove or disprove the hypothesis.
Observations/Results • Organization	• Observations are presented but are difficult to understand.	• Observations are evident but need to be presented in a chart or diagram for clarity and organization.	• Observations are clear and organized.	• Observations are presented in a clear, organized, identifiable manner, using charts, diagrams, or paragraphs.

FIGURE 5.9
A RUBRIC FOR A SCIENCE LAB *(continued)*

Dimensions	Novice	Apprentice	Practitioner	Expert
Observations/Results *(continued)*				
• Relevance	• Observations/results need to relate to hypothesis with evidence of observable facts.	• Observations/results are indirectly related to the hypothesis with facts that need to be stated more clearly.	• Observations/results relate to hypothesis.	• Observations give evidence of observable facts that strongly relate to the hypothesis.
• Supporting details	• Observations/results need to have details that clarify the observations and support the procedures, materials, and hypothesis.	• Observations/results include details, but the details need to be explained further to more fully support the procedures, materials, and hypothesis.	• Observations/results contain details that support the procedures, materials, and hypothesis.	• Observations/results contain a variety of details that support the appropriateness of the procedures, materials, and hypothesis.
Conclusion • Understanding	• Presents written conclusion but needs to communicate what has been learned about how procedures and observations prove or disprove the hypothesis.	• Communicates what has been learned, but thoughts need to relate to how the procedures and observations prove or disprove the hypothesis.	• Communicates what has been learned about how procedures and observations prove or disprove the hypothesis.	• Communicates what has been learned about how procedures and observations prove or disprove the hypothesis with a significant level of insight.
• Use of data	• Conclusions are drawn, but the relationship to the data is not clear.	• Conclusions are supported by data but need to be explained.	• Conclusions are supported, but the scope of the conclusions are broader than what the data support.	• Conclusions are supported by data with explanations, and all data are accounted for.
• Supporting details	• Explanations need to be written and supported with relevant details.	• Details are limited and need to be relevant to the procedure and hypothesis.	• Relevant details help support part of the conclusions.	• Explanations are supported with a variety of relevant details.

Source: Developed by Lisa J. Boerum. Copyright © 1997 by Center for the Study of Expertise in Teaching and Learning (CSETL). Used with permission.

FIGURE 5.10
A RUBRIC FOR "DOES EGYPT QUALIFY AS A GREAT CIVILIZATION?"

Dimension	1	2	3	4
Opening Statement	–Reader is uncertain about author's position. –Sentence is simple and lacks adjectives or superlatives.	–Author states position. –Attempt to captivate audience is clumsy and needs revision.	–Author states opinion clearly. –Adjectives and superlatives help interest reader enough to motivate him or her to continue.	–Author states opinion in a manner that compels reader to continue.
Content	–Information and supporting sentences are irrelevant or conflicting. –Inaccurate information is included. –Correlation between culture and civilization is not established. –Words and language used do not mirror expectations of grade level. –Lacks specific Egyptian vocabulary. –No closing statement.	–Sentences lack sufficient information to adequately support opinion. –Basic correlation between culture and civilization is made. –Lacks consistency in using appropriate language and words. –Specific Egyptian vocabulary is used sporadically. –Closing statement is used.	–Author supports opinion with relevant facts and information. –Author demonstrates a correlation between culture and civilization citing specific examples linking the two. –Specific Egyptian vocabulary is used throughout the essay. –Closing statement sums up argument.	–Uses comparisons, analogies, and examples to support opinion. –Understanding of relationship between culture and civilization is so evident that reader easily grasps concept. –Specific Egyptian vocabulary used appropriately throughout the essay. –Closing statement leaves reader with a sense of validity.

FIGURE 5.10
A RUBRIC FOR "DOES EGYPT QUALIFY AS A GREAT CIVILIZATION?" *(continued)*

Dimension	1	2	3	4
Mechanics	–Spelling mistakes make reading difficult. –Does not use capital letters to start sentences. –Little variety in types of sentences. –Absence of punctuation. –No paragraphs. –Contains incomplete sentences, fragments, or run-ons.	–Numerous spelling mistakes indicate a need for revision. –Fails to capitalize in all appropriate places. –End marks are omitted or not used properly. –Sentences need additional variety. –Paragraph structure needs improvement. –Must find and correct incomplete sentences or run-on sentences.	–Minor spelling mistakes. –Capitalizes first words of sentences and proper nouns. –End marks are used accurately. –Appropriate use of paragraphs and indentation. –Contains only complete sentences.	–Flawless spelling and grammar. –Uses a variety of punctuation marks accurately. –Excellent use of paragraphs adds to fluidity of essay.
Neatness	–Handwriting is difficult to decipher. –Numerous mistakes crossed out inappropriately. –Lacks final copy expectations.	–Handwriting is acceptable, but improvement is needed. –Final copy attempt is evident but additional revision is needed.	–Handwriting is excellent. –Minor errors with one line cross outs.	–Typed. –No errors.

Source: Developed by Rick Hinrichs. Copyright © 1999 by Center for the Study of Expertise in Teaching and Learning (CSETL). Used with permission.

FIGURE 5.11
A WRITING MECHANICS RUBRIC THAT VIOLATES CONTENT GUIDELINES

Dimension	1	2	3	4
Punctuation and Capitalization	Meaning not clear because of mistakes in punctuation and capitalization.	Some mistakes in punctuation.	Few mistakes in punctuation.	No mistakes in punctuation.
Spelling	Words unreadable because of spelling.	Some mistakes in spelling.	Few mistakes in spelling.	No mistakes in spelling.

Content

The following guidelines apply to the content of all rubrics:

• The rubric describes both content (what students should demonstrate that they know, think, or can do) and form (what their products, performances, or processes should look like).

• The descriptors are written in clear and specific terms, avoiding relative or evaluative language.

• The rubric shows consistency from level to level—that is, skills and indicators are present at each level.

• Qualitative adjectives, when used, are supported by specific indicators.

• The wording for lower levels describes what is evident; that is, students can read about what is evident in their work and not primarily about what is missing.

• The top level is the standard in the field and not the expectations that teachers have for a specific group of students.

Figure 5.11 is part of a rubric for writing mechanics that violates several of these guidelines. For example, the descriptors rely on evaluative and relative language, and the wording for the lowest level addresses only what is missing.

Structure or Form

Rubrics should conform to the following guidelines for structure or form:

• Levels are sequenced in a continuum that supports instruction.

• Levels progress from the least developed to the most developed, or vice versa.

• The distance between each level of performance is fairly equal.

Figure 5.12 is part of a rubric for organization in writing that does not follow these guidelines. The figure includes two possible revisions to correct some of the flaws in the original rubric. One of the revisions focuses on the writing, and the other focuses on the effect of the writing on the reader. Which revision is preferable is a matter of opinion.

FIGURE 5.12
A WRITING RUBRIC THAT VIOLATES GUIDELINES FOR STRUCTURE OR FORM

Dimension	1	2	3	4
Organization		Shows organization.	Writing has a beginning, middle, and end.	Writing is well organized and thoughtfully sequenced (beginning, middle, and end).
1st possible revision of dimension	• *Can't tell beginning, middle, end.* • *Order of events is confusing.*	• *Beginning, middle, and end can be inferred.* • *Some events are out of order.*	• *Beginning, middle, and end are clear.* • *Events are in order but lack transitions.*	• *Beginning, middle, and end are clear.* • *All events are in order.* • *Transitions guide reader from one event to another.*
2nd possible revision of dimension	• *Order of events confuses the reader.* • *The reader is unable to tell the beginning, middle, and end.*	• *The reader can identify the beginning, middle, and end but is sometimes confused about the order of specific events.*	• *The beginning, middle, and end are clear, and events are in order.* • *Transitions would help the reader follow from event to event.*	• *The beginning, middle, and end are clear.* • *Events are sequenced with clear transitions that allow the reader to easily follow from event to event.*

Layout

The following guidelines apply to the layout or mechanics of rubrics:

• The rubric has a title.

• The dimensions (of an analytic rubric) are labeled.

• The dimensions (of an analytic rubric) are defined by either a sentence or a question.

• The dimensions (of an analytic rubric) are listed in priority order or in a logical order (that is, from the beginning to the end of a process).

• The type is readable.

• The layout is user friendly—it includes sufficient white space and uses bullets or a grid or table format.

• The rubric includes space for comments by teacher and/or student.

What Are Common Problems of First-Draft Rubrics?

The following are some of the problems commonly seen in the first draft of a rubric:

- The task or project is inappropriate for a rubric.
- The rubric gives insufficient attention to content and overemphasizes form.
- The descriptors are not clustered in logical groups.
- The descriptors are not specific.
- In an analytic rubric, some rubric dimensions are missing.
- The dimensions are not sufficiently prioritized or logically presented.
- The rubric relies too much on quantitative terms (e.g., *several, numerous*) to define levels of performance.
- The rubric relies too much on adjectives to distinguish between levels.
- The rubric is wordy but vague.
- The lowest level is described primarily in terms of missing elements.
- The top level does not describe the real-world standard, or it does not help students to see the relationship between the top level and the real-world standard.
- The attributes for product and process are mixed together.
- The rubric combines developmental or norm-referenced language with criterion-referenced descriptions (e.g., "above average in reaching the standard").

The rubric in Figure 5.13 has several problems. For example, the Description dimension relies on quantitative terms to describe the different levels. The author does not consider the depth of information presented or the connections made between things like religion and values. Another significant problem is that the Description dimension mentions involving the audience, which is a matter of form rather than content. The author should consider creating a dimension that discusses teaching strategies or strategies for addressing different learning modalities. The reader may notice other problems in addition to these.

What Roles Can Students Play in Developing and Using Rubrics?

Teachers can involve students in the development and use of rubrics by asking them to do the following:

- Identify attributes of quality for a product or process.
- Cluster attributes.
- Draft a rubric.
- Think about and discuss the importance and weighting of attributes.
- Give feedback on the strengths and weaknesses of a rubric.
- Refine a rubric to make it more useful.
- Use a rubric to self-assess a product or performance.
- Use a rubric to assess anonymous student work.
- Use a rubric for peer assessment.

Teachers may encounter certain problems when developing rubrics with students. For example, students may become rather anxious when asked to

FIGURE 5.13
A RUBRIC FOR AN ORAL PRESENTATION ON A CULTURE (ILLUSTRATING COMMON PROBLEMS WITH RUBRICS)

Dimension	5	4	3	2	1
Content: Connection	Is able to make meaningful connections with the culture and describe how these connections have changed or affected their life or beyond.	Is able to make meaningful connections with the culture by discussing similarities and differences.	Is able to make a meaningful connection with the culture but is unable to connect it with their life.	Is able to make a superficial or obvious connection that didn't really need to be said (e.g., Chinese have New Year, we have New Year).	Makes no connections at all.
Content: Description	Describes the cultural beliefs, values, arts, customs, traditions, religion of the chosen area and provides some audience involvement; allows teaching of the different pieces.	Describes the cultural beliefs, values, arts, customs, traditions, religion of the chosen area.	Describes most of the cultural beliefs, values, arts, customs, traditions, religions of the chosen area.	Describes some of the cultural beliefs, values, arts, customs, traditions, religion of the chosen area.	Describes none of the cultural beliefs, values, arts, customs, traditions, religion of the chosen area.
Organization	Presents a clear, sequential presentation with clear, appropriate transition.	Presents clear ideas, in order, but has difficulty with the flow and transition.	Presents ideas clearly but a piece(s) could be better placed elsewhere.	Presents ideas but is either unclear or out of order.	Presents ideas but is unclear and out of order.

(continues on next page)

FIGURE 5.13
A RUBRIC FOR AN ORAL PRESENTATION ON A CULTURE (ILLUSTRATING COMMON PROBLEMS WITH RUBRICS) *(continued)*

Dimension	5	4	3	2	1
Visual Aids	Visual aids are clear, precise, eye-pleasing, and used at the appropriate time to link effectively with the presentation.	Visual aids are used at the appropriate time to link with the presentation but are less clear and precise.	Visual aids are used at inappropriate times.	Visual aids are not appropriate for the presentation.	No visual aides are used.
Eye Contact	Eye contact is used effectively throughout entire presentation to gain and hold the audience's attention.	Eye contact is used throughout entire presentation but does not effectively gain and hold the audience's attention.	Eye contact is made randomly with the audience and other areas of the room.	Eye contact is made with areas of the room but not with the audience.	Eyes are down throughout presentation.

develop a rubric for a kind of work they know little about. They also may have little to say if the process of developing the rubric is not preceded by a careful analysis of good examples or models. Finally, students may not feel free to use their imaginations in developing a rubric if the teacher is too focused on a single way of depicting quality.

One way to help students understand a rubric that they did not help develop is to show them *exemplars* (samples that illustrate the top level of performance or quality) and *anchors* (samples that illustrate the intermediate and lower levels of performance or quality). Lisa McEvoy, a primary school teacher in the Rockville Centre School District in New York, developed the rubric for a science lab shown in Figure 5.14 (pp. 58–59). It includes examples of student work at each level for a lab on food coloring and water, which is unrelated to the lab being assessed. Although the lab topic in the examples is different, the students can understand the different levels of performance by looking at the examples of the lab for food coloring and water.

Another way to help students use a scoring rubric is to develop visual aids for the different levels of quality. This is especially important for young learners who may have some difficulty reading the text of a rubric. Mary Ellen Cuiffo, a primary school teacher in the Farmingdale School District in Farmingdale, New York, incorporated a picture into her rubric for a story presentation (see Figure 5.15, p. 60).

Teachers of primary school students can also create folders of work depicting the different levels of performance of a specific product or performance. Students can review the folders before developing their own. Finally, teachers of very young children can create symbols to represent different levels of quality, rather than using words or phrases.

How Can Teachers Develop a Rubric by Themselves?

Developing a rubric basically involves two steps: drafting and refining.

The Drafting Stage

The drafting stage relies on the teacher's imagination and prior exposure to the product, performance, or process for which the rubric is being created. Here are the steps in the drafting stage of the development process:

Step 1: Identify and list all the attributes and indicators that make a quality and authentic performance, process, or product. Think about both content and form. If student work is available, look at several exemplars to describe what quality looks like.

Step 2: Write a brief rationale for this assessment, spelling out why this assessment is important and what it shows about what students know, are able to do, or value.

Step 3: Cluster these attributes and indicators into possible groups or categories and label each group with a heading. Each group becomes a *dimension* in the rubric.

Step 4: Rank each group or dimension in priority order in terms of importance or value, or determine the order that will be most useful for students as they work.

Step 5: Decide the number of levels the rubric will have and what order they will appear in (for example, reading from left to right, a rubric can go from the lowest level to the highest, or vice versa). The list you made in Step 1 will be the basis for one level of your rubric.

Figure 5.14
A Holistic Science Lab Rubric with Benchmark Samples

Science Expert (4)	Science Teacher (3)	Science Student (2)	Scientist in Training (1)
You made a prediction of what you thought would happen based on what you know.	You made a prediction of what you thought would happen based on what you know.	You made a prediction of what you thought would happen.	Your prediction is missing or is hard to understand.
You explained why you made this prediction.	You drew a picture that explains what you saw. You also wrote words that help to explain your picture.	You drew a picture that explains what you saw. You might have written a few labels for your picture.	You drew a picture of what you saw.
You drew a detailed picture that explains what you saw. You also wrote words that help to explain your picture.	You told what you discovered from this experiment using an explanation.	You told what you discovered from this experiment.	You wrote a question you still have.
You told what you discovered from this experiment, using clear, specific explanations.	You reflected on the experiment by asking questions that it made you wonder about or questions that you still have.	You reflected on the experiment by asking questions it made you wonder about.	*Food Coloring and Water* How will the food coloring and water interact?
You reflected on the experiment by asking some questions it made you wonder about or questions you still have.	*Food Coloring and Water* How will the food coloring and water interact?	*Food Coloring and Water* How will the food coloring and water interact?	I predict it will turn blue.
Food Coloring and Water How will the food coloring and water interact?	I predict the food coloring will take a long time to mix with the water unless we stir it. I think we will be able to see the food coloring drip down to the bottom of the cup.	I predict the food coloring will take a long time to mix with the water unless we stir it.	Here is a picture:
I predict the food coloring will take a long time to mix with the water unless we stir it. I think we will be able to see the food coloring drip down to the bottom of		Here is a picture:	Does the same thing happen to red color?
		I was right! It looked really cool, like sand art! I learned that food coloring and water	

FIGURE 5.14
A HOLISTIC SCIENCE LAB RUBRIC WITH BENCHMARK SAMPLES *(continued)*

Science Expert (4)	Science Teacher (3)	Science Student (2)	Scientist in Training (1)
the cup. When we dye eggs at home for Easter, we use food coloring and water and that is what happens. Here is a picture: I was right! The food coloring didn't mix with the water until Joseph stirred it! It sank to the bottom almost right away. It looked really cool, like sand art! I discovered that food coloring drops to the bottom of a glass of water when you first add it. It floats around slowly by itself and you can really see the interaction. Then when you stir it, the water and color mix together so much you can't tell which is which. I wondered why the food coloring didn't just stay on the top like oil drops do. Is it heavier? I also wonder if the food coloring will ever totally mix with any help from people.	Here is a picture: I was right! The food coloring didn't mix with the water until Joseph stirred it. It looked really cool, like sand art! I discovered that water and food coloring will mix when you stir them together. I wondered why the food coloring didn't just stay on the top like oil drops do. Is it heavier? I also wonder if the food coloring will ever totally mix without any help from people.	mix. I wonder if the food coloring will ever totally mix without any help from people.	

Source: Developed by Lisa M. McEvoy, Rockville Centre School District in New York. Copyright © 1997 by Center for the Study of Expertise in Teaching and Learning (CSETL). Used with permission.

Figure 5.15
A Rubric for Primary Grades

You planned what you said very well.

You used your imagination and lots of details.

You used great words.

You remembered to use capital letters and periods all the time.

You could read all of your story.

You planned what you said.

You used your imagination a little, and you used some details.

You used good words.

Sometimes you remembered to use capitals and periods.

You could read most of your story.

Your plan needs to be clearer, or you forgot to plan.

You didn't use enough details.

Some of your words are confusing.

You forgot to use capitals and periods.

You could read only a little of your story.

Source: Mary Ellen Cuiffo, Farmingdale School District, Farmingdale, New York. Drawings by Kathleen Perry, Farmingdale School District, Long Island, New York.

Step 6: Fill in the information for the levels of the rubric by describing the behaviors, characteristics, or qualities of a task/project/performance that exhibits

- a high performance to be expected from the best students in the class
  - world-class standards
  - average or acceptable standards
  - less than adequate standards
  - unacceptable standards or an initial performance level

Write each of the levels on a separate sheet of paper, and don't look at the wording of one level before writing the next one. This makes it easier to imagine the work at a specific level rather than relying on comparative language like "less creative" or "five facts instead of seven." Also, develop the four levels for one dimension before moving to another. Don't worry about parallel structure of language until the rubric is finished. Initially it is advisable to write a four-level rubric because it is difficult to define more than four levels without student work at hand. Later, in the refinement stage, a comparison of the range of work students have produced against the number of levels originally identified can determine whether additional levels are warranted.

The Refinement Stage

After the teacher has used the rubric once and has received student work guided by the rubric, the development process can go through a refinement phase. An analysis of student work informs the process at this point. Here are the steps in the refinement stage of the rubric development process:

Step 1: Review the rubric to be sure it includes the important component parts and follows the guidelines for quality listed earlier.

Step 2: Ask a peer for feedback.

Step 3: Have students use the rubric to assess a work in progress. Ask students which parts of the rubric work well and which parts are troublesome and why. Keep notes for revisions. Label any new drafts that may be created.

Step 4: Use the rubric on a pile of student work. While using the rubric, make notes about which parts work well, which parts are problematic, and why.

In the process of refining rubrics, it helps to keep in mind that the rubric development process takes time, isn't always neat, and can be difficult at times. Furthermore, the process of refining rubrics is endless. A rubric will never perfectly match the range of what students produce. Finally, a rubric is likely to get better and better as teachers and their students become more sophisticated and proficient users of the kind of work depicted by the rubric.

How Can Teachers Develop Rubrics Using State Standards and Indicators?

Teachers can develop rubrics using state or other standards by studying their standards documents and searching for performance indicators that would be evident in student work stemming from a specific assignment. If state standards have been written for different subjects, teachers should look for indicators in several sets of standards, always including language arts or English because the standards in those subjects apply to all assignments that require any form of communication. After identifying all pertinent performance indicators, teachers can cluster these indicators and label them, much as they would if, instead of using the standards, they had simply brainstormed the qualities of a specific assignment. If the state standards are benchmarked for different grade levels or grade clusters, teachers can use the indicators under the elementary or lower-grade benchmarks to define the lower levels of the rubric, the indicators under the intermediate benchmarks to define the middle levels of the rubric, and the indicators under the commencement benchmarks to define the upper levels of the rubric.

Using standards in the development of rubrics has several advantages. First, the standards often provide specific language defining the quality and rigor in students' work. Second, by incorporating the standards and the accompanying performance indicators into their rubrics, teachers can clearly show the alignment of their assessments with the standards.

How Do We Know That Rubrics Are Good Enough?

Figure 5.16 (pp. 63–64) is a rubric that teachers can use to evaluate the quality of their rubrics and to improve them. It is adapted from a "rubric for rubrics" developed by Angela DiMichele Lalor, a former teacher in the William Floyd School District in Long Island, New York, and Elizabeth Bedell, a science teacher in the William Floyd School District, Long Island, New York.

Regardless of their quality at a specific time, rubrics are never finished. They get better every time a teacher uses them and then refines them based on the assessment of students' work. Multiple drafts of rubrics provide explicit evidence that the teacher and the student are becoming more sophisticated about what is being scored by the rubric. In addition, just because a rubric is developed with students does not mean it will adequately serve their needs; likewise, just because a

teacher-developed rubric worked well with a particular group of students does not mean that it will work with another group. All students need to engage meaningfully with rubrics before they can use them. They need to translate the language in the rubric into their own words or use it in low-pressure situations, such as to score anonymous work or outside samples, before they can use it to score their own work.

Recommended Resources

Danielson, C., & Marquea, E. (1998). *A collection of performance tasks and rubrics: High school mathematics*. Larchmont, NY: Eye on Education.
This book supports the National Council of Teachers of Mathematics (NCTM) standards by discussing different types of assessment for mathematics and expanding on the benefits of performance assessment. It contains a collection of 21 performance tasks and rubrics that are problem-centered. Included are step-by-step procedures for creating a performance task and a rubric to evaluate student work and student learning. Each problem has student anchors and exemplars ranked 1 through 4 as they were scored with the rubric.

Kuhn, T. M. (1997). *Measure for measure: Using portfolios in K–8 mathematics*. Portsmouth, NH: Heinemann.
The target audience for this book is elementary and middle school mathematics teachers. In a mere five chapters and less than 120 pages, the author clearly defines the purposes and types of portfolios in education; the process of reshaping the culture in one's classroom to accept the changing role of student and teacher when portfolios are used; the use of rubrics to evaluate individual assignments and portfolios, addressing parents' concerns and questions; and issues that arise when portfolio assessment is implemented. The author makes a strong case for educators becoming aware of how their assessment system aligns with the curriculum and instructional practices. The author does not make light of the additional time that teachers will need to evaluate portfolios but does make reasonable suggestions for how to go about

FIGURE 5.16
A RUBRIC FOR RUBRICS

	4 Master Rubric Maker	3 Intermediate Rubric Maker	2 Apprentice Rubric Maker	1 Novicer Rubric Maker
Dimensions—The headings or titles of each category	• Each dimension clearly identifies and explains the teacher's main ideas, expectations, and required components of the assessment. • Dimensions are placed in a purposeful order, allowing students to understand the relative emphasis of each component of the assessment.	• Each dimension identifies the teacher's main ideas and required components of the assessment. • Dimensions are placed in a logical order without any reference to the relative emphasis of each component of the assessment.	• Dimensions digress from the main ideas of the assessment and prevent a full understanding of all the required components of the assessment. • Dimensions are placed in an order that contradicts the logical placement of each component of the assessment.	• Dimensions are unconnected to the main ideas and components of the assessment. • Dimensions for each component of the assessment are missing or not properly labeled.
Descriptors—The statements used to describe each heading	• Descriptors are written in concise and clear terms that completely describe the dimensions and provide an anchor of what is expected from the students at each level. • Emphasis is on precise, concrete, and descriptive statements with all levels written in terms of what is evident.	• Descriptors are written in clear terms that convey teacher expectations. • Emphasis is on accurate statements that avoid missing or negative terms. • Descriptors are identified and present at each level.	• Descriptors are vague and difficult to understand, leaving too much to student interpretation. • Combination of descriptive as well as quantitative, value-laden statements (e.g., "2 examples," "good," "abundant"), with lower levels written in terms of what is not evident.	• Descriptors are unrelated to dimension. • Quantitative, value-laden, and subjective statements (e.g., "some," "1 example," "fair"), with overemphasis on what is not evident. • Descriptors are missing.

(continues on next page)

FIGURE 5.16
A RUBRIC FOR RUBRICS *(continued)*

	4 Master Rubric Maker	3 Intermediate Rubric Maker	2 Apprentice Rubric Maker	1 Novicer Rubric Maker
Descriptors— *(continued)*	• Descriptors are clearly identified and present at each level.		• Descriptors are difficult to identify and may be missing at different levels.	
Content—The information contained in the descriptors	• Content of the rubric provides a detailed account of the assessment at each level.	• Content of the rubric provides an overview of the assessment.	• Content of the rubric provides a partial view of the assessment.	• Content of the rubric is unrelated to the assessment.
Levels—The scale of the rubric (e.g., in this rubric, 1 through 4)	• Descriptors provide scaffolding for students by describing an evenly graduated progression toward excellence. • Level titles use terms that show respect and dignity for the learner/user while accurately critiquing performance on the task. • The number of levels is dictated by concrete, nontrivial differences in student performance.	• Descriptors at adjacent levels progress in even steps toward achievement. • Level titles focus learner/user on the grade and identify the levels of achievement (e.g., proficient). • The number of levels is determined by external constraints (grades, outside agencies) rather than distinctions in student performance.	• Unequal difference between the descriptors at adjacent levels hinders student self-evaluation and correction. • Level titles focus learner/user on grade (4, 3, 2, 1). • The number of levels does not permit sufficient distinction in quality of student work.	• There is no difference between descriptors at adjacent levels. • Level titles at the lower end are insulting or demeaning to the person rather than descriptive of student work. • The number of levels leads to artificial, nonexistent, or trivial differences in descriptors.

Source: Developed by Angela DiMichele Lalor and Elizabeth Bedell, William Floyd School District, Long Island, New York. Copyright © 1999 by Learner-Centered Initiatives, Ltd. Used with permission.

this process in the chapter on rubrics. In fact, the chapter on rubrics should be required reading for any teacher.

Lazear, D. (1998). *The rubrics way: Using multiple intelligences to assess understanding*. Tucson, AZ: Zephyr Press.
This book does an excellent job of relating multiple intelligence theory to assessment practices. It is also a useful book for anyone seeking a foundation in multiple intelligence theory. It spans current evaluation models while making a case for alternative assessments, a bias centered upon multiple intelligences. To the author's

credit, *The Rubrics Way* offers rubrics to fit all eight learning styles. Especially interesting are the chapters on creating student intelligence profiles and then using the profiles to extend the students' intelligences by playing on their strengths. Lazear includes a chapter that features 11 activities that bring the intelligences together. He also includes a chapter that investigates other approaches to creating and using multiple intelligence rubrics. Finally, he examines definitions of authentic assessment and illustrates different assessment formats. Charts and diagrams reinforce key points. The text is fully documented and includes a noteworthy bibliography.

Portfolios: A Window into Students' Thinking and Learning

6

[**Essential Question:**
Who Are We as Learners?

This chapter describes student portfolios as windows into students' thinking and learning. Many of the tools used to determine what students know and are able to do fall short of truly uncovering what lies behind such knowledge and skills. Portfolios look beneath the surface and discover what students think, how they think, what they value, and who they are. When used appropriately, portfolios are the most comprehensive tools for documenting students' growth, efforts, and achievements. They provide evolving images of students' work and, when accompanied by students' reflections, enable readers to witness what students think about themselves as learners.

This chapter defines and justifies the use of portfolios and describes different kinds and uses of student portfolios. It also provides guidelines for initiating their use and for sharing them with parents and with other teachers. Appendix C provides a module for designing portfolio assessments.

What Is a Portfolio?

A portfolio is a collection of student work that exhibits the student's efforts, progress, and achievements in one or more areas. This collection is special because it is guided by a clearly established purpose and has a specific audience in mind. Unlike a district folder of students' writing in different grade levels, this collection represents a personal investment on the part of the student—an investment that is evident through the student's participation in the selection of the contents, the criteria for selection of the items in the collection, the criteria for judging the merit of the collection, and the student's self-reflection.

Portfolios can provide a multidimensional view of students' development and achievement. They can be designed to show evidence of effort (all drafts leading to a completed product); corrections of test errors; progress (baseline or sample of work done before the teacher's intervention and a parallel exit task); and achievement (examples of best work).

Why Should Teachers Use Student Portfolios?

Portfolios supplement the existing array of assessment tools teachers have at their disposal. There are at least eight good reasons for teachers to consider using them.

1. *Documentation of students' best work, effort, and growth.* Portfolios depict learning in more profound ways than other assessments because they show the interplay among effort, growth, and achievement. This allows students and teachers to demystify grades and put learning in context.

2. *Focus on authentic performance, or knowledge-in-use.* Portfolios include all kinds of evidence of learning, not just the kind derived from traditional assessments, such as tests and quizzes. A portfolio might include, for example, a photograph of a three-dimensional project or a summary of feedback the class gave a student for an oral presentation. In fact, portfolios are well suited to document students' ability to use what they have learned.

3. *Student access to structured opportunities for self-assessment and reflection.* Portfolios enable teachers and students to create spaces for students to reflect on their progress, learning, and achievement. Such reflection could be a letter to the reader, an introduction to the portfolio, or reflective statements that accompany the various portfolio entries or artifacts. A portfolio without a student's reflection is not really a portfolio, but rather a collection of work that is hard to decipher without commentary from its author.

4. *Evidence of thinking.* Related to reflection and self-assessment is evidence of students' thinking about the merits and shortcomings of their work, as well as the processes they followed to complete tasks and projects. Such thinking enables teachers to discover misconceptions, identify gaps in understanding, and learn about how different students engage with the same assignments.

5. *Thick description of student learning.* Unlike any other kind of assessment, portfolios are multi-layered. They reveal students' learning processes along with multiple manifestations of such learning. For instance, a portfolio that includes a carefully selected collection of a student's writing for different purposes and audiences over a one-year period reveals more than the sum of all of the student's writing for the year. There are at least two reasons for this. First, not all the writing that the student produces during a term is equally reflective of ability. Second, when students compile their portfolio, they spend time deciding on the pieces that support their attainment of desired learning outcomes. That decision-making process reveals much about how well they understand and accept the quality attributes of their work.

6. *Validation of a developmental view of learning.* Portfolios allow teachers to witness growth. When portfolios include early samples of student work as well as end-of-year samples, teachers and students can assess growth over time.

7. *Choice and individualization for students and teachers.* When teachers encourage students to assume responsibility for the identification and selection of artifacts that provide evidence of learning, portfolios become self-portraits of students as learners, each one as unique as the student who compiled it.

8. *Opportunities for conversations with different audiences.* Given that portfolios are purposeful collec-

tions of work that tell a story of a student's learning, they can be shared with a variety of audiences in ways that students' notebooks, journals, and binders cannot. Such audiences may include parents, counselors, and support staff.

What Are the Kinds of Portfolios and What Purposes Do They Serve?

There are at least five kinds of portfolios—and dozens of variations. The *showcase* portfolio is designed to document achievement or the potential to achieve. This portfolio is akin to the artist's portfolio. The *development* or *growth* portfolio is designed to show the student's growth or change over time. The *process* portfolio aims at documenting the process by which work is done, as well as the final product.

The *transfer* portfolio is derived from the preceding portfolios and is used to communicate with students' subsequent teacher, school, or admissions office when students move from one educational setting to another. For example, a high school student may extract her best thinking, writing, and creative pieces and add them to her college application as evidence of the quality of her work.

All of these kinds of portfolios can be assessed and graded, provided that the teacher and students identify specific performance criteria against which they can be measured.

The *keepsake* portfolio serves as a repository of students' favorite or memorable work. This kind of portfolio is much like the scrapbooks or photo albums that adults compile to record family events or vacations.

Most teachers combine the various kinds of portfolios in ways that serve their needs and those of their students.

What Kinds of Artifacts Do Portfolios Include?

Even though portfolios can vary widely, they often share some common pieces. These include a letter to the reader explaining the portfolio; a table of contents; periodic goal statements and strategies for meeting goals; reflections on the work included; drafts and final versions of at least one of the pieces included; self- and peer-evaluations accompanied by teacher- and student-completed checklists. The letter to the reader is an essential part of the portfolio because it introduces the student to the reader and provides the reader with a road map for the review and appraisal of the portfolio contents.

What Are Some of the Issues to Think About When Designing a Portfolio?

One of the issues for teachers to consider when designing a portfolio is whether the portfolio will be structured to provide evidence of students' attainment of specific learning outcomes or standards, or whether it will be driven by curriculum content. In an outcome-driven portfolio, teachers ask students to select entries for outcomes such as the following:

• *Perseverance*. Work that shows that you are persistent; a project that took at least one week to complete, with an explanation of the steps taken to complete it; or a paper that includes drafts and revisions, additions, or other changes, along with a justification for those changes.

• *Mathematical representation/communication*. Work in which you use a graph, table, chart, or diagram to inform others; or a write-up of a complex problem with an explanation of all the steps you used to solve it.

• *Reading/writing.* A piece of writing for which you could have changed the ending to improve it, along with a description of the changes that could be made; work that shows you have improved as a reader of literature; a log that shows the range of books you have read; a selection of book notes from different kinds of books.

• *Communication in another language.* A piece of work that shows that you can initiate and sustain face-to-face conversations in French; a translation of a dialogue you heard in German; or a letter written to a pen pal in Spain.

• *Collaboration.* A sample of work done with at least one other person in class, accompanied by a description of how each group member worked together and evidence of the group members' individual contributions to this work.

• *Collaboration/historical understanding.* A project that you developed with someone else in class to demonstrate the relationship between the past and the present, along with a description of your own and your partner's contributions to this work.

• *Analytical skills.* Writing that analyzes a situation or a document.

As the preceding list indicates, in a standards- or outcomes-based portfolio, the teacher provides the students with a list of outcomes or standards, or generates such a list with them. The students choose among their work to select the pieces that provide the best evidence of their progress toward or attainment of these outcomes.

On the other hand, in a curriculum- or content-driven portfolio, the teacher uses the curriculum or text to decide on the work that should be included as evidence of students' learning. For example, a science teacher may ask students to compile the following artifacts: one lab write-up per marking period, two end-of-unit tests, three consecutive

days of notes, and their first and last research reports. As a result, curriculum-driven portfolios tend to be much more standardized than outcome-driven portfolios.

Although most teachers prefer the idea of outcome-driven portfolios, they often begin their use of portfolios with tightly controlled curriculum-driven portfolios. The reason for this apparent paradox is that teachers often want to maintain a tight grip of the portfolio structure and selection activities until they and their students become comfortable with them and can develop familiar routines for incorporating them into their assessment repertoires.

A related issue teachers should consider when designing portfolios is the extent to which the portfolio will be driven by the teacher or by the students. That is, who will decide what goes into the portfolio—the teacher, the students, or both? An outcome-based portfolio tends to be more student-driven than a curriculum-driven one in that the student has more freedom to choose appropriate evidence in the former than the latter. However, even an outcome-based portfolio can be teacher-driven when the range of pieces from which students can select is very limited. This would be the case if a teacher asked students to select a piece that shows that they are artistic and students had only one or two opportunities during the year to produce anything that called for an artistic representation.

The following questions can help teachers test the degree to which they are willing to assume more or less control of their students' portfolios:

• If you were in a position to develop a collection of your students' work that captures their growth and achievement in your class(es), what five artifacts would you select?

• If you asked your students to compile the same type of collection, what do you think their collection would include?

• What would you learn about your students from your collection?

• What would you learn about your students from their collection?

• What are the key differences and similarities between your list of artifacts and theirs?

• How do you feel about the differences and similarities?

In designing a portfolio, teachers also need to decide if the portfolio will be graded. If it will be, they need to determine how it will contribute to the student's grade. This is an important decision because the grading of the portfolio requires that teachers determine how a collection of work is different from the sum of the individual pieces. If such pieces have been graded before their inclusion in the portfolio, teachers need to decide what the portfolio grade will be based on. If, on the other hand, teachers decide not to grade the portfolio, then they must determine if incentives or conditions are needed for students to value the compilation and reflection involved in creating the portfolio.

What Are Some Guidelines for Beginning to Use Portfolio Assessment?

Portfolios can be like good wine: they improve with time. Unlike good wine, however, portfolios are not meant to sit still. Rather, they become increasingly refined as teachers systematically use and examine them. Here are some guidelines for getting started:

• *Decide upon a primary purpose and audience for the portfolios.* If you cannot make a decision among two primary audiences or purposes, develop two different portfolios. Some teachers like the idea of having students create a school portfolio and a home portfolio.

• *Identify the learning outcomes that will drive the portfolio design.* Decide if the curriculum will be outcome-driven or curriculum content–driven. Select the outcomes or curriculum areas that the portfolio entries will seek to make evident.

• *Start small and focused.* Begin with a short list of outcomes or with a narrow scope for content. Limit the use of portfolios to one class if the intent is to use the portfolio for evaluation purposes. Allow one or two years to experiment with different kinds of portfolio entries and approaches. Do not expect to develop a comprehensive understanding and management of portfolios the first year you use them. After all, they comprise a purposeful collection of work that means a lot more than the assembly of discrete papers and objects.

• *Inform parents of your plans to use portfolios and include a schedule or time line for sharing students' work.*

• *Create your own portfolio and use it to model the use of portfolios.* Model everything you want students to do with their portfolios, beginning with describing the reasons behind your entries. You can create a portfolio that showcases you as a learner or a curriculum and assessment designer, or one that incorporates your history as a teacher, the range of roles and responsibilities you have, or your goals and strategies to attain them.[1]

---

[1]Teachers can greatly benefit from the development and use of professional portfolios. See Martin-Kniep, G. (1999). *Capturing the wisdom of practice: Professional portfolios for educators.* Alexandria, VA: Association for Supervision and Curriculum Development.

• *Incorporate the portfolio into your classroom routines.* Set up a place and a filing system for portfolios (filing cabinets, milk crates, small cartons, or pizza boxes, for example). Identify possible portfolio contents (either by yourself or with students) and a schedule for selecting them. Link contents to the learning outcomes you identified in the second guideline. Decide which contents will be required and which will be optional and identify who will select the contents.

• *Generate criteria for selecting and judging contents* (preferably with students). Integrate criteria into classroom activities. Encourage students to make selections on a regular basis (once per month or marking period) and discuss ways in which they can update their portfolios. Promote the idea of students sharing their selections and reasons with other students. Even if you decide not to grade the portfolio, you need to be clear about what you are looking for and about the qualities that differentiate portfolios. Begin with a working portfolio and shift later to a showcase and growth portfolio.

• *Incorporate reflection and self-assessment into the portfolios.* Reflection is central to the development and use of portfolios. It needs to be modeled, cultivated, and taught. Take the necessary time to help students recognize what you mean by thoughtfulness, and make reflection a habit in your classroom. Have students assess their work regularly, using criteria generated in class. Showcase good and poor examples of portfolio choices and reasons.

• *Give students ownership of their portfolios.* Student-centered portfolios allow teachers to learn about how students think about their work and what they value. They enable students to monitor their growth and achievement and to use their portfolios to generate and refine learning goals.

• *Share portfolios.* Portfolios allow teachers and students to share their work in ways that others can understand and learn from. Encourage students to share their portfolios with their peers and with their parents, either individually or as a group (at a Portfolio Night or at student-led portfolio conferences, for example). Develop a strategy for allowing teachers in other grades to access and use student portfolios.

What Role Does Reflection Play in Portfolio Assessment?

Reflection is a critical attribute of portfolios. In fact, without it, portfolios become encoded collections that only their developers understand. The following is a list of reflective questions that teachers can use to guide students' selections for their portfolios:

• How do the pieces in your collection illustrate what you can do as a writer?

• What do you notice when you compare your earlier work to work you produced later in the year?

• What makes your most effective piece different from your least effective one?

• What goals did you set for yourself? How well did you accomplish them?

• What are you able to do that you couldn't do before?

• What are your reading goals for the next semester?

• In what ways has your ability to solve problems changed?

• In what ways are your reading and writing connected? How does one affect the other?

• If you had to pick the one thing I did that helped you the most as a learner, what would it be?

• Describe the experience and process of putting your portfolio together. What have you learned about yourself as a learner, a writer, a reader?

Chapter 7 includes ideas to help teachers help their students become more reflective. Appendix C provides tools for designing portfolio assessments.

Recommended Resources

Burke, K. (1997). *Designing professional portfolios for change*. Arlington Heights, IL: IRI/Skylight Training and Publishing.

This book offers a hands-on, step-by-step approach for documenting change through the use of professional portfolios. The author defines the differences among inservice, professional development, and staff development, and then describes a variety of professional portfolios. Chapters are dedicated to resources, data collection, collaboration, selection and organization, reflection, evaluation, and conferences and exhibits. The book includes black line masters that structure various components of a portfolio, and the complete portfolio of a fictitious 11th grade English teacher.

Danielson, C., & Abrutyn, L. (1997). *An introduction to using portfolios in the classroom*. Alexandria, VA: Association for Supervision and Curriculum Development.

This book provides an overview of three types of portfolios: working, display, and assessment. The authors outline the purposes of each portfolio and their benefits and challenges, as well as the overall management of using portfolios in the classroom. This book is a good resource for teachers beginning or considering portfolio assessment. It also serves as a good reference for portfolio-related terminology, and its user-friendly organization with many subheadings makes it a quick reference as well.

Graves, D. H., & Sunstein, B. S. (1992). *Portfolio portraits*. Portsmouth, NH: Heinemann.

The authors have compiled a unique look at portfolios through the personal "hands-on" experiences of several educators as they grow in their understanding of the meaning and use of this new tool. Readers are given a chance to experience insights into portfolios as both an evaluative and instructional vehicle that is closely aligned to self-evaluation and literacy itself.

Hewitt, G. (1995). *A portfolio primer*. Portsmouth, NH: Heinemann.

This book describes how Vermont schools develop classroom portfolios. It is user-friendly and contains a number of student samples.

Johnson, B. L. (1996). *The performance assessment handbook: Portfolios and Socratic seminars*. Princeton, NJ: Eye on Education.

This book calls for teacher-centered classrooms and inquiry-driven curriculum. This shift demands new forms of assessment that are based on student performances of knowledge. Portfolio assessment and Socratic seminars are recommended as especially powerful learner-centered strategies. The author suggests starting with standards and developing rubrics and scoring criteria to define these standards. The book is easy to read, with many examples at the high school level.

Kent, R. (1997). *Room 109*. Portsmouth, NH: Heinemann.

This book shares the stories, learning, and relationships of students and teacher in a responsive, theme-based, portfolio-building high school language arts class. Motivation for learning is grounded in relationships created by the author and labeled as a "learning family." The book begins with the first day of school, when students rejoice over the announcement of "no tests" and builds to the crescendo of Portfolio Day, when students realize that they have worked much harder and learned much more in Room 109 than they ever intended. The book is enjoyable reading and includes examples of the various required portfolio pieces plus life experiences and attitudes expressed throughout the year.

Kuhn, T. M. (1997). *Measure for measure: Using portfolios in K–8 mathematics*. Portsmouth, NH: Heinemann.

In a mere five chapters and fewer than 120 pages, the author clearly defines the purposes and types of portfolios in education; the process of reshaping the culture in one's classroom to accept the changing role of student and teacher when portfolios are used; the use of rubrics to evaluate individual assignments and portfolios, addressing parents' concerns and questions; and issues that arise when portfolio assessment is implemented. The author makes a strong case for educators to become aware of how their assessment system aligns with the curriculum and instructional practices. The rationale for adding portfolio assessment to the other assessment tools in a mathematics class is woven throughout the book. The author does not make light of the additional time that teachers will need to evaluate portfolios but does make reasonable suggestions for how to go about this process in the chapter on rubrics.

Martin-Kniep, G. O. (1999). *Capturing the wisdom of practice: Professional portfolios for educators.* Alexandria, VA: Association for Supervision and Curriculum Development.

The author explains how teachers and administrators can improve their practice and career potential by developing and using a professional portfolio. This introductory guide has all the steps and strategies needed to cre-

ate a professional portfolio. It covers ways to start a portfolio and make sure it reflects abilities and accomplishments; what teachers and administrators should include in a portfolio; and types of portfolios that are best for researchers, professional developers, or curriculum designers. It provides examples of effective portfolios and systemwide portfolio efforts and discusses four areas of portfolio specialization: learner, researcher, professional developer, and curriculum and assessment developer.

Porter, C., & Cleland, J. (1995). *The portfolio as a learning strategy.* Portsmouth, NH: Heinemann.

This book profiles two high school teachers' experiences with portfolios over a three-year span. It incorporates the teachers' motivations for using portfolios and the strategies they used to implement them. It also includes numerous student samples. Although the author underscores student reflection, the book mainly includes examples of student reflection of final products rather than reflections on their processes and initial learning.

Reflection: A Key to Developing Greater Self-Understanding

7

[**Essential Question:**
How Do We Learn?

We have traditionally told students what *we* see and what *we* value—very often at precisely the point in their learning where they should be discovering what *they* see and what *they* value. In doing so, we have reduced the likelihood that students will use past experiences in writing to shape subsequent experiences. We have eliminated the valuable opportunities for students to learn about themselves and about their writing—and for us to learn about them.

—Roberta Camp (1992)

When students assume responsibility for their own learning, they reflect on their accomplishments, evaluate their work, decide on where changes are needed, define goals, and identify sound strategies for attaining them. If students are to become thoughtful individuals who can assume responsibility for learning, they must be taught how to analyze and evaluate their work. Teachers must help them define realistic yet challenging goals for their continued learning and show them appropriate strategies to attain those goals. This chapter is intended to help teachers understand the role of reflection and self-assessment in the learning process and to incorporate self-evaluation and monitoring activities into their classrooms.

What Is Reflection and Why Is It Important?

Webster's unabridged dictionary defines *reflect* as "to think seriously; contemplate; ponder." Reflection is a critical component of self-regulation. Self-regulated learners are aware of the strategies they can use to learn and understand when, how, and why these strategies operate. They can monitor their own performance and evaluate their progress against specific criteria. They can recognize improvement and identify strategies for dealing with challenging situations. They know how to choose appropriate goals, can develop and implement reasonable plans, and can make appropriate adjustments if unforeseen circumstances occur. In short, self-regulated learners are strategic.

Reflection is intrinsic to many of the learner-centered practices described in this book. Reflection can enhance authentic assessment as students determine how to grapple with real problems and challenges. Reflection supports the use of portfolios because it becomes the means through which students can study themselves and their work. It is also tied to rubrics because it enables students to refer to explicit performance criteria to monitor their learning. Finally, reflection is a staple of action research as teachers ponder, study, and evaluate their practices.

As with other learner-centered practices, reflection requires that teachers provide students with time to think about their learning. However, even though reflective activities take time, they also save teachers time. They increase the efficiency of student learning by enabling students to be strategic learners. They decrease teachers' workloads because students assume greater responsibility for collecting and evaluating their work and that of their peers. Reflective activities also provide teachers with critical feedback about the limitations of their curriculum, facilitating its subsequent revision.

Reflection is needed throughout the learning process. Teachers can ask students to reflect on their knowledge, skills, attitudes, and dispositions. Students can evaluate the merits and shortcomings of their products, processes, or performances. They can determine the extent to which the learning opportunities teachers provide them with help them learn. They can also set achievement goals and strategies and evaluate their attainment. All of these are necessary and essential reflective activities.

How Can Teachers Get Students to Invest in and Value Reflection?

To get students to be reflective and value the process of thinking about their learning, teachers need to practice and value reflection themselves. When teachers value their own and their students' reflections, the processes of learning become as important as its products, and the focus of evaluation moves from something that is done at the end of a project or a marking period to something that occurs throughout the school year.

Teachers need to help all students reflect, but some students will need more help than others. For example, many students, particularly young children or students categorized as "at risk," need to know that teacher approval or grades are not the only or best source of evaluation of their work.

Teaching students to be reflective is an ongoing process, not an event. It requires access to models, practice, and time. The following conditions increase the meaningfulness of reflection for students:

• Students need to feel safe about sharing what they think.
• Reflective activities should be comprehensive, purposeful, and meaningful.
• Reflective questions, prompts, and responses should be specific.
• Reflection needs to be modeled and standards-based.
• Reflective activities should be targeted toward an audience.

• Reflective activities should be ongoing and should be practiced.

Students need to feel safe about sharing what they think. This condition is present when teachers make a habit of celebrating mistakes and reminding students that mistakes generate true opportunities for learning. It also occurs when teachers share their own thinking, successes, failures, frustrations, and concerns and remind students that everyone is a learner. The following entries from student journals suggest that students in a class feel safe:

> [Reflective prompt from teacher] Explain what you are still confused about or need more understanding with in social studies.
>
> I need more understanding with map skills. I think there are many ways of having a clearer understanding of map skills. The maps in the packet are confusing.
>
> I get confused with longitude and latitude. I didn't learn it from the homework assignments.
>
> I am a little confused on dates and times in history. I feel I need a little more understanding about why and when things happened.

Reflective activities should be comprehensive, purposeful, and meaningful. Reflection is enhanced when it addresses multiple and ongoing aspects of students' work or learning. Teachers can ask students to reflect on what they know about a topic that is about to be introduced, how they are grappling with content being taught, and what they have learned about a topic after a unit is completed.

Regardless of the timing or focus of a reflective activity, its meaningfulness should be self-evident and intrinsically connected to the learning experiences that precede or follow it. For example, stu-

dents may reflect on the aspects of writing they struggle with, so the teacher can use this information to shape writing activities to individual needs. Joanne Picone-Zocchia, a former 6th grade language arts teacher in the West Islip School District in West Islip, New York, asked her students to assess themselves at the beginning of the year. The following is how one of her students responded to the questions "Do you see yourself as a writer? Why or why not?"

> I do not see my self as a writer. The only thing I do well is the idea part. No, I don't wish to better. You can't help because I don't want to be a writer. But I would describe my self as a good silent reader. Picturing the story in my head. Long words. Reading out loud.

Given the information provided by the student, Joanne can continue to probe this student's resistance to writing and develop an individual plan that addresses his needs.

Not all students respond equally well to any given reflective activity. To increase the meaningfulness of reflective prompts and strategies for responding to them, teachers could ask students to generate their own reflective questions or to choose those that are relevant to them from among several options. Prompts for reflection will vary from activity to activity. The prompts for a math activity may not necessarily be the same as those for an art or social studies or integrated project.

Reflective questions, prompts, and responses should be specific. The questions "How have you grown as a writer?" and "How have you grown in your ability to write a thesis statement?" are very different in terms of specificity. For students who are very young or who have not had much practice with reflection, it is important that teachers use specific questions rather than general ones. Specificity also concerns the extent to which students are encouraged to refer to particular sections or parts of their work to support their responses to reflective prompts. The following fill-in-the-blank entry, from another student in Joanne Picone-Zocchia's class, is a good example of specificity. Notice the student's proposed revisions to a piece of writing.

> I wish I had the chance to change *My ghost story* which I wrote in *October*. If I could, I would *expand on my vocabulary and sentence structure*. *To expand on my vocabulary I would fix this sentence:*
>
> Now Joey was back at home, he just lay in bed all alone.
>
> to
>
> When Joey returned home, he just lay in bed all alone.
>
> To expand on my sentence structure I would turn this:
> As Joey lay in his bed frozen
> to this:
> It was a dark and gloomy night, as Joey lay in his bed, frozen in fear.
> I would also like to work on varied sentence beginnings, because I keep saying Joey at the beginning of every sentence. To fix my story I would also give supporting details to support my paragraphs.

Enabling students to be specific in their self-assessments is not easy. It is not uncommon for students to give teachers one-word or one-line responses to the first reflective questions teachers ask them. For example, in response to the question "Why is this your best piece of writing?" students might say, "Because I like it"; "Because I got an A"; or "Because it's long."

Students need to acquire a language that facilitates reflection. This language is both descriptive, requiring students to elaborate on their thinking, and evaluative, requiring them to assess their work.

One of the strategies for helping students be specific in their reflection is to generate with them a list of attributes they can use when assessing their work. Shari Schultz, a 6th grade teacher from the Hilton School District in Hilton, New York, generated two lists with her students. One list, a Success Scale, helped the students assess how successful they were in an activity (see Figure 7.1). The second list, the Engaged Learner Checklist, helped them assess the merits and shortcomings of a project they had participated in (see Figure 7.2).

A related strategy involves asking students to place brief descriptors next to the work that best illustrates that work. For example, a mathematics teacher can ask students to review their notebook pages and to place Post-it notes with phrases such as "effective use of graphs, charts, tables"; "clear explanation of process used in solving problem"; "multistep problem solved in two different ways" on the pages that best illustrate those qualities. After marking their pages, students can refer to the pages that have the most Post-it notes to select and describe their best work.

Reflection needs to be modeled and standards-based. Teachers can model reflection by reflecting with students and sharing their reflections. They can show students models of quality reflection and discuss with them why the models are good. They can show models of poor reflection and discuss how the models might be improved. Finally, they can ask students to interview their parents or other adults to find out when and how they reflect.

It is always easier for students to reflect and self-assess when they have participated in the identification of criteria for good reflection, when the teacher uses those criteria to respond to students, and when students use the criteria when reflecting and evaluating peers. Figure 7.3 (p. 80) is a list of composite criteria generated by students in several 6th grade classes.

FIGURE 7.1
A TEACHER- AND STUDENT-GENERATED SUCCESS SCALE

Success Scale

Directions: Check one for this activity

_____ EXTREMELY SUCCESSFUL
   I feel good about this.
   I am proud of this work.
   This is my best work.
   I met my goal(s).
   I put forth my best efforts.
   I'm excited about my work.
   I'm capable of doing my best.

_____ MODERATELY SUCCESSFUL
   I feel okay.
   I could've done better.
   I did close to my best.
   I almost met my goal(s).
   I could've put more time into it.

_____ NOT VERY SUCCESSFUL
   I could've done a lot better.
   I could've worked harder.
   I didn't care about it.
   It wasn't my best.
   I'm disappointed in my work.
   I'm upset with my work.
   I didn't meet my goal(s).
   I didn't put much effort into it.

Source: Shari A. Schultz and 6th grade students in the Hilton School District, Hilton, New York.

Figure 7.4 (pp. 81–83) is a rubric for reflection generated by a group of teachers in Long Island who were participants in a three-year project to design learner-centered curriculum and assessments. They later used the rubric to help their students identify and use the attributes of reflection.

Reflective activities should be targeted toward an audience. Students can self-assess better when their reflections are directed toward a specific audience they perceive to be interested and caring. This audience can include the teacher, the student, other students, parents, and others. The following reflection is by a 6th grader in Margaret Brizzie's class. Margaret is a language arts teacher in the Webutuck School District in Webutuck, New York. This student clearly describes how he sees himself as a reader, writer, and thinker and shows that he is able to self-assess.

I think I'm a very good reader. I like to read science-fiction books usually. When I read I usually read for about an hour a day and I finish books in about a week. The books are usually about 350 to 400 pages. On good days I read about 50 pages in the day. If I find a word that is hard to pronounce I take a word that sounds like it. If there is a name like Tas, I say it like Taz because I think it is a bad name. I usually read series of books like the DragonLance books. If there is a book report that is the only time I stop reading the series I'm reading. When I'm doing research I usu-

---

**FIGURE 7.2
A TEACHER- AND STUDENT-GENERATED CHECKLIST**

ENGAGED LEARNER CHECKLIST

For this project/activity I . . .

___ had choices
___ was involved in competition
___ was challenged
___ worked outside
___ was entertained
___ worked in groups
___ could use my imagination
___ could get rewards
___ could act
___ could work all day
___ was doing something "real life"
___ could do it without the teacher
___ got something out of it at the end
(learning experience)

___ got to interact with others
___ could be with my friends
___ was excited to work on it
___ liked doing it
___ felt I was good at it
___ was satisfied
___ enjoyed working on it
___ had fun
___ had a variety of activities
___ could be creative
___ was interested in what I did
___ did something not too hard but difficult

Source: Shari A. Schultz and 6th grade students in the Hilton School District, Hilton, New York.

---

ally only use encyclopedias, unless I need to use a magazine. I always read the directions to a worksheet. For a game I sometimes read the directions. That is how I think I read.

I think I'm a very good writer. I usually write fiction or science-fiction stories. I write 1 to 5 pages in a story and 200 to 2000 words a story. I can see improvement in my writing since the beginning of the year. My stories are longer, my paragraphs are better, and my wording has gotten better too. My spelling is usually right and I use my punctuation right to. I never let anybody read my stories until the story is done. That is how I write my stories.

I think that I'm an okay thinker. My memory is not that good but if I have to memorize some thing I always try. When I get ideas they usually come when I'm writing my stories. That is how I think I think.

Reflective activities should be ongoing and should be practiced. Teachers need to provide opportunities for students to practice reflection regularly and to share their reflections with one another. The more people reflect the better they get at understanding themselves as learners. Reflection should be accompanied by honest and continuous feedback that students can use to improve their learning.

[**FIGURE 7.3**
STUDENT-GENERATED CRITERIA FOR A GOOD REFLECTION

A good reflection—

1. Is honest.
2. Answers the questions or responds to the statements.
3. Contains examples and details to support opinions and thoughts.
4. Helps the person who wrote it understand himself/herself better.
5. Informs the audience (teacher, classmates, self, etc.). It gives useful information.
6. Shows that the person really thought about the question before writing down a response. You can tell the response is really what the person thinks.

7. Shows personal perspective.
8. Is easily understood by the reader. It is free of spelling mistakes as well as confusing language that would interfere with a reader's ability to understand what was written.
9. Is based on what the person believes or thinks about what is asked.
10. Shows thinking.

What Kinds of Prompts Can Teachers Use to Encourage Students to Reflect?

By using prompts, teachers can ask students to reflect about many aspects of their learning and work. Here are some suggestions for creating various kinds of reflective prompts:

• Write two reflective prompts to accompany a student project—one that focuses on the project itself and one that focuses on the process.
• Write a prompt to accompany a test.
• Write three prompts for a unit of study—one for the beginning of the unit, one for the middle, and one for the end.
• Write two prompts that students can use to select work for their portfolio.
• Create a monthly reflection activity that will be ongoing in the classroom, and write reflective prompts for the first month.

• Write a reflective prompt to use with parents.
• Write a reflective prompt for a homework assignment.
• Write a reflective prompt for group work.
• Write a reflective prompt that will help students assess the teaching of specific content or skills.

See Appendix D for examples of questions and prompts to use for lessons, individual pieces of work, grading and tests, the learning process, the process used to develop specific work, the impact of teaching on the student, and goal setting. You will notice that, in general, prompts and questions that seek to help students think about and assess their learning need to be specific and intrinsically connected to the work or learning that a student is doing or has recently experienced.

FIGURE 7.4
A REFLECTION RUBRIC

Dimension	4	3	2	1
Writing	Communicates effectively to identified audience. Writer's voice is evident throughout with the use of jargon-free and real language. Thoughts are well organized and presented with no ambiguity. The writing is focused throughout the reflective piece. Style of writing is rich. Writer supports analysis of questions, problems, concerns, with theories, comparisons, conclusions, metaphors, analogies, and clearly linked examples to elaborate on ideas and enhance meaning.	Communicates effectively, although a specific audience is unidentified. Writer's voice is evident in different parts of the material. Scattered use of jargon. Thoughts are organized and logically presented. Some portions of the material are more developed and focused than others. Style of writing is apparent. Writer supports selected part of material with questions, problems, concerns, theories, comparisons, conclusions, examples, metaphors, and analogies.	Communication is directed at a general audience and needs elaboration. Writer's voice is clouded through the use of jargon and formulaic language. Thoughts are either too general, random, or are not presented in a manner that can easily be followed. The material presented is scattered with gaps and needs transitions. Style of writing is generic. Writer presents questions and descriptions in general terms with few or unconnected supporting examples, analogies, or comparisons.	Communication is incomplete and unelaborated. Writer's voice cannot be discerned either because the communication lacks focus or development, or because the use of jargon is excessive. Thoughts are presented in very general or incomplete terms. Style of writing is not discernable. There are obvious gaps and needs for additional information in the forms of examples, questions, comparisons, analogies, and specific concerns.
Self-Awareness/ Process	Clearly identifies and illustrates strengths, weaknesses, confusions, and areas of inquiry by specifically stating areas and reasons for	Identifies strengths, weaknesses, confusions, and areas of inquiry by stating areas in which they occur, although does not explain rea-	Identifies general strengths, weaknesses, and confusions but does not explain or illustrate these. Conclusions can be inferred	Reflection addresses strengths, weaknesses, or confusions in vague or incomplete terms. Concluding statements are missing.

(continues on next page)

FIGURE 7.4
A REFLECTION RUBRIC *(continued)*

Dimension	4	3	2	1
Self-Awareness/ Process *(continued)*	sons why they occur. Draws perceptive conclusions from self-evaluations and differentiates issues and questions that have been resolved from those that need further thinking or inquiry.	their occurrence. Draws general conclusions from self-evaluations but does not differentiate resolved from unresolved issues or questions.	but are not specifically stated. Reflection does not include new questions or issues.	
Risk-Taking	Honestly communicates successes and failures with concrete examples; provides illustrations of learning processes and expectations; effectively defines and clarifies values, thoughts, and feelings regarding self, students, and/or nature of work. Clearly demonstrates a willingness to change and learn, even to the point of operating differently than the perceived norm.	Communicates successes and failures openly but in general terms. Describes learning processes, expectations, values, thoughts, and feelings regarding self, students, and work conditions. Willingness to change and learn can be inferred although is not explicitly mentioned.	Refers to successes and/or failures in broad and unsubstantiated terms. Learning processes, expectations, thoughts, and feelings regarding work, self, and students are only partially addressed. Willingness to change or learn cannot be determined from information presented.	References to successes, failures, thoughts, feelings, or processes regarding work, self, or students are missing or too ambiguous to be understood. Reflection does not include information that suggests a willingness on the part of the writer to learn or change in any way.

FIGURE 7.4
A REFLECTION RUBRIC *(continued)*

Dimension	4	3	2	1
Goal-Directedness	Goals for curriculum, instruction, and/or assessment practice are specific and derived from a thorough analysis of current performance and priorities. Suggestions for self-improvement are clearly linked to a review of the strengths and weaknesses of current work. Proposed goals seem ambitious but attainable.	Goals for curriculum, instruction, and/or assessment practice are specific and are linked to current practice and priorities. Suggestions for self-improvement are generally related to perceived strengths and weaknesses. Proposed goals seem either too ambitious or not ambitious enough.	Goals for curriculum, instruction, and/or assessment practice are general and/or unrelated to analysis of current practice. Suggestions for self-improvement and proposed goals are too general or too tentative, and are divorced from stated strengths and weaknesses.	The relationship between perceived goals and current practice cannot be established either because the analysis is too superficial or has not been completely carried out. Goals are not stated in attainable terms.

Source: Developed by Giselle O. Martin-Kniep, Diane Cunningham, and faculty from the Long Island Performance Assessment Project.

What Does Reflection Look Like?

All students can reflect, although younger students often lack some of the language needed to express their thoughts. The samples that follow are from students at various grade levels. Some of them include the reflective activities and prompts, indicated in italicized type, that led to the students' responses. Teachers can use these samples to model and discuss reflection with their students.

1st Grade

The first four samples included here depict a range in the specificity and degree to which students addressed the teacher's prompt. First grade teachers could use these samples to discuss the importance of elaboration when students reflect.

Look though all your journal pages for October. Choose one page that you think is very special. It should be a page you would like people to remember about your work in 1st grade. Tell why you chose this page in your journal. Tell what was happening on the page. [Teacher records the students' answers over a four-day period.]

Today we have music. It was a special picture because it was the truth. It means really real. I really like music.

I liked it because I used a lot of detail. It was my best picture in October. It was almost Halloween, and I like drawing Halloween pictures before Halloween.

It's my first time going on the big rollercoaster at Adventureland. I keep going on it. It feels good.

All my pictures looked scribbled and that's the one that looked nicer. There's words with the silver and clouds. I was doing the weather. These puddles look like real slippery ones, and I'm slipping on them. I used the green that looked like real grass.

The following portfolio letter shows that 7-year-olds can understand and apply the meaning of elaboration. Erin's use of examples to substantiate her claims is both purposeful and very effective in helping readers know she has assessed her growth:

Portfolio letter

Dear reader,

I know how to read and write better than I did last year. I know how to read more books than I did las year.

I can read compound words like treehouse and swingset. I can read one chapter book. I can cover up half the wor to find out what it is.

I know how to write to have better handwriting than I did last year. I know how to spell more word like share and things.

I would like to know how to spell more words and read more books.

Love Erin

2nd Grade

This student reveals an awareness that waiting can be judged on the basis of its impact on the reader.

I selected this piece because it had my best evaluation and almost nobody had questions. The idea is very exciting and interesting to the reader. It has a great beginning and ending. It has all the fairy tale criteria. My story makes sense. It creates crystal clear pictures for my reader. It has many neat and detailed illustrations. It has almost no proofreading marks.

How was reading different the second time we taped?

This reflection shows that this student has internalized multiple criteria for oral reading:

> I read with fealings.
> I read with lowdnis.
> I read with out mstamake.
> I read with happnis.

3rd Grade

Students' learning goals can reveal much about their perceptions of what is important, as is evident in the following reflection:

> My goals for November are:
> I will try to stay organized.
> I will look at the teacher.
> I will write neatly.
> I will write complete sentences.
>
> *React to your first week in 3rd grade: likes, dislikes, surprises, questions, etc.*

Reflections can also reveal how students make sense of the contexts that surround them—for example, in the following statement:

> In 3rd grade I have the best teacher. Our class pet is fish. Its fun 3rd grade because we have my teacher.
>   We are up stairs. I have 27 kids in my class. I would like to learn cursive hand writing. We have little libery in our class.

4th Grade

The internalization of quality criteria is clearer and more sophisticated in the following statement than in the previous example by a 2nd grader. These two examples could be presented together and used with students to clarify or teach the meaning of "elaboration."

> *What are the characteristics of good writing?*
>
> Well, when you use imagery it makes the reader picture it. When you use big words

you impress the person and also good grammar helps the reader to understand. Using similes makes it wonderful writing. Using different words with the same meaning for example, "nice" and "beautiful." Describing lots of things. Don't use many "thens." Use lots of adjectives.

6th Grade

This is a good example of the use of evidence to support the selection of work for a portfolio. It underscores the importance of having student reflections in a portfolio. Without them, it would be difficult for readers to understand the reasons supporting students' reflections of their work.

> *How have you grown as a writer?*
>
> When I look at my Ghost Story and my Jed Story, I can really see my growth as a writer. I've changed in some important ways. I've given the story more detail and description. In the ghost story I had description, but in the Jed story, I gave even more. For example, in the ghost story:
>   "The grass looked like it hadn't been cut for years."
>   And in the Jed story:
>   "The rain hit hard on the roof like marbles hitting a hard wood floor."
>   Now I don't know about you, but I saw real change. As you can see, my Ghost story and my Jed story are two excellent examples of my growth as a writer.

8th Grade

The following reflection reveals how a student associates her work with herself. She clearly sees her portfolio as a presentation of self and not just a collection of work:

> . . . Anyway, I've put my blood and sweat into this portfolio. It expresses who I am as a

real person. Not just a student. I know how very hard it really is to think of another person with real thoughts just like you have . . . that's what I've tried to do all year. Express myself in writing to a point so that if someone reads my portfolio, they will know who I am.

9th Grade

The following excerpt underscores how reflective prompts and questions can open a window into students' minds. This student's explanation of the criteria she has used to assess her work reveals the value she places on effective use of chronology in writing. Such criteria would never be known by the teacher had he or she not taken the time to ask the question.

Self-Assessment

Style/clarity/format:

An 8 would be the grade I deserve in this category. I purposely tried to avoid a factual, essay like report. I really tried to add in the necessary facts in an honest way, so as not to disturb the flow of the piece. I also thought up the story-line myself, after doing extensive research on Colombia's drug problem. The reasons that I gave myself an 8 rather than a 9 or a 10, is because I still feel like there might be some confusion left over after one reads my story. This is because my story covers many years, and is constantly referring to the past, and present events in this person's life. To me, it is very clear who is speaking. However, people seem to still be confused. Through my drafts, I tried to smooth the edges around these time changes, and give little clues to tell the reader whether its past or present. Unfortunately, I don't think that I was 100% successful in my attempts to make the distinction crystal clear.

10th Grade

The following student's reflection of her unsatisfying piece shows that she has made a connection between her intent and motivation and the quality of her work. It is also an exemplary reflection in its use of evidence within the "work" to support a student's assertion of its value.

The Unsatisfying Piece

I am very unhappy with this piece for one reason in particular: I asked for it. Being the "creative" writer that I was, I asked if our class could do something a little more stimulating than an essay; say a short story or something. The teacher brought out a topic especially for me; an essay called "Guess who is coming to dinner . . ." The premise was that one could invite five characters to a party. One was supposed to write about their conversation, seating arrangement, and stay true to the characters' true personalities. Unfortunately, this was to be done in a stricter format than I imagined. My plans were rather shattered, and so I wrote an essay without imagination, inconsistent with the characters' views, and essentially just to get it done. Needless to say, I was very unsatisfied with it.

I had planned on writing in almost a play style; with the characters speaking freely. . . . The limits of the assignment confined my imagination. I wrote the essay without any imagination, even though I invited very interesting people (Jim, Hester Prynne, Miniver Cheevy, Starbuck, and Georgiana). For the first half of the piece, I didn't use any direct quotes. My characters all *would've* said this or *could've* done that. The paragraphs that did have quotes were no better. The characters were talking about love, marriage, and devotion in a weak and uncreative way. Indeed, most of the time I had Miniver and Hester insulting each other.

My feeble attempt at humor (Miniver puking on the guests) was in poor taste and missed the entire point of the poem . . .

The last example of student reflection shows that students can provide teachers with valuable information about the merits and shortcomings of their lessons and units by communicating what they have learned from them.

12th Grade

The difference between my pre-test and post-test is very simple. I did not know anything about the Vietnam war before this unit. All I knew was that it was one of the wars the Americans fought in. Previous to this unit, I had seen *Ms. Saigon* on Broadway. This musical is about the Vietnam war. The main thing that I got from the show was that there were many men who went over to Vietnam and fell in love with a woman there, and many of them had their children.

After going through this unit, I now know that there is much more to the war than just some babies that were half American and half Vietnamese. There were many men killed. . . . the most of any war. Many men had severe psychological problems after the war. After they left the war, they carried it with them forever.

I'm glad we did this unit, because I really did not know anything before. That is why it is easy for me to compare my two tests.

Recommended Resources

Cambourne, B., & Turkell, J. (Eds.). (1994). *Responsive evaluation: Making valid judgments about student literacy*. Portsmouth, NH: Heinemann.
This book discusses different ways to respond to student learning. It encourages teachers to expand upon their ideas about student evaluation and has an excellent chapter on creating communities of learners and making assessment a systematic process. The book also shows ways for young children to engage in self-evaluation.

Egan, K. (1986). *Teaching as story telling*. Chicago: University of Chicago Press.
The author offers an alternative to the generally accepted elementary school curriculum that begins with the concrete and builds toward the abstract. After questioning some of the educational principles on which the typical curriculum is based, Kieran Egan suggests instead an elementary school curriculum based on what he calls "The Great Stories of the World Curriculum." He suggests that teachers use his Story Form Model, which begins with questions such as "What is most important about this topic?" "Why should it matter to children?" "What is effectively engaging about this topic?" "What binary opposites best catch the importance of this topic?" and "What content most dramatically embodies the binary opposites, in order to provide access to the topic?"

In opposition to the view that young children do not understand abstract ideas, the author argues that young children have a strong comprehension of ideas such as loyalty and betrayal, honesty and cheating, freedom and tyranny. In fact, he states that these are the very ideas that excite children's intellects and about which children really care. When the classroom teacher employs ideas such as the binary opposites listed above in nonfiction stories related to the curriculum, students will learn because they become actively engaged in the lesson. Egan also discusses how using the Story Form Model for lesson design can help instill in students wonder and awe for the everyday, workaday world. *Teaching as Story Telling* provides a smorgasbord of food for thought.

Paris, S., & Ayres, L. (1994). *Becoming reflective students and teachers with portfolio and authentic assessment*. Washington, DC: American Psychological Association.
This book presents a practical, structured approach to the implementation of portfolios and ongoing authentic assessment in the classroom. The authors address three themes revolving around the idea of reflection. The first is the notion of reflection in and of itself and the healthy, constructive thinking that takes place within

oneself when contemplating classroom practice, curriculum, assessment, instruction, and meaningful learning. Whether it is the teacher, student, or parent doing the reflecting, the authors stress that it is indeed a powerful process that drives self-directed and enhanced learning for each individual. The second theme emphasizes the importance of ensuring that opportunities for reflection are deliberately planned for as part of daily or weekly instruction and assessment activities, and that this self-assessment takes place individually *and* within small discussion groups (consisting, for example, in the case of student reflection, of the teacher, student, and parent). The third theme is that self-assessment promotes personal development—that reflecting about one's acquisition of knowledge and skills will foster positive developmental outcomes.

Action Research: Asking and Answering Questions About Practice

8

[
Essential Question:
How Do Questions Teach?

Diane Cunningham

The concept of action research, or teacher inquiry, is sometimes intimidating and often a mystery. However, many teachers have undertaken projects that involve the elements of action research, including finding a focus, generating questions, collecting data, and making sense of what the data reveal. Although their work may have fit the definition of action research, perhaps it wasn't labeled as such. This chapter demystifies action research and provides a picture of what the process looks like, starting with the question that is asked most often.

What Is Action Research?

The word *research* conjures up a process that many educators don't want to embrace. But as Glenda Bissex points out in *Seeing for Ourselves*, "a teacher researcher doesn't have to study hundreds of students, establish control groups, and perform complex statistical analysis" (Bissex & Bullock, 1987, p. 3). She defines a teacher researcher as "an observer, a questioner, a learner and a more complete teacher" (p. 4). Teachers need to recognize that being a teacher researcher, or doing action research, fits naturally with what they already do in the course of their day, week, and year.

Action research is a process of asking important questions and looking for answers in a methodical way. The questions are meaningful; that is, the researcher wants or needs to know the answers to the questions, and the questions are closely connected to the teacher's work. Action research, in this sense, is very practical and grounded in the day-to day work of the researcher. One way that it is different from traditional or scientific research is that the researcher is not removed from what is being studied, but rather is a part of it. Teacher researchers are researching their own problems or new practices. The research is modest, manageable, and, again, directly related to daily work. Also, the work is often part of an inservice course or district-sponsored teacher study group. These characteristics explain why action research can be so meaningful and empowering for teachers.

What Does the Action Research Process Look Like?

Action research is very much a recursive process, not unlike writing and thinking. Researchers must go through three stages: planning, implementation, and analysis and reflection. However, researchers often leap back and forth between the stages. Each stage involves researchers in specific actions and behaviors:

Stage 1—Planning
- describing actions
- articulating a rationale for the actions
- drafting research questions
- reading related literature
- planning for implementation
- deciding on data collection strategies
- creating a time line

Stage 2—Implementation
- taking action
- documenting actions taken
- observing and collecting data about the results
- reading related literature

Stage 3—Analysis and Reflection
- analyzing data
- reflecting on results and process

- articulating answers to research questions
- asking new questions

A problem, challenge, or the desire to try something new is the impetus for educators to design an action research project. In the *planning stage*, researchers draft questions, revise questions, draft plans, and revise plans. Planning is informed by reading related literature and by past experiences. At this point researchers may or may not have ideas or hunches about the answers to these questions.

As the *implementation stage* begins and researchers carry out the new actions, they also begin to collect data. They must track what they do and the results of what they do. Even as the researchers work, they sometimes revise their plans and revise their questions. Their work is informed by the work of others as they continue reading in the area of their research. Sometimes answers begin to emerge as data are collected, but more often they emerge later, in the analysis and reflection stage.

During the *analysis and reflection stage*, researchers look closely at the data collected, analyze it, and reflect on what it means in relation to the questions asked. This final stage is when the real learning comes. As researchers work to make sense of the information they have collected and articulate the answers to their questions, they make meaning from their work.

The action research process, like writing, can be satisfying, confusing, unpredictable, hard, easy—or all of these. But because it is grounded in a practitioner's work and is meaningful, it is worth sticking with. It is exciting to see answers to questions emerge—even if the answers are a surprise and if answers emerge to questions the researcher never posed.

How Can an Educator Plan a Meaningful Action Research Project?

To get started on the planning stage of an action research project, educators can follow these five steps:

1. Identify the topics or ideas that the research may be related to.
2. Describe the actions that will be taken and studied and articulate a rationale.
3. Write action research questions related to the actions.
4. Create a plan for data collection.
5. Create a timetable to guide the research.

Appendix E includes a module to guide action researchers through each of these steps. The module is a refinement of work done by author Stephen Kemmis. The sections that follow here further explain the steps and describe the action research plans of three educators: Lisa Boerum, a special educator in the Sag Harbor School District in Long Island, New York; Sue Cox, director of curriculum and technology for the Penn-Harris-Madison School Corporation in Mishawaka, Indiana; and Patrick Kruchten, a multiage classroom teacher in the Hilton Central School District in Hilton, New York.

Step 1: Identify the Topics or Ideas

Many educators begin action research because they have a problem or challenge. Others begin a project because they want to try something new or modify existing practice in some way. Either place is a good starting point.

Example 1: Lisa Boerum. Lisa's jumping-off point for this action research project is a challenge that she knows she will face in the coming school year, namely helping students monitor, assess, and assume responsibility for their own learning.

> I am anticipating students who are more at risk than those I had last year. Several incoming 6th graders have demonstrated apathy toward learning, difficulty in persisting through the process to complete tasks, and have demonstrated a marked weakness in reading and writing which has affected them in all academic areas. The specific problems include apathetic student learning, low self-expectation, low performance level, and lack of ownership.

Example 2: Sue Cox. Sue has designed an action research project around two challenges related to a major initiative in her district.

> For several years the role of computers, access to the Internet, and the use of technology has been a top priority of our district's strategic plan to prepare students for the future. Millions of dollars have been spent to acquire hardware, software, local and area networks, and Internet access in all of our schools.
>
> Problems:
>
> 1. Now that our schools have this technology, school board members and members of the community are asking, "Does the technology have an impact on teaching and learning?" While we have collected some data regarding teachers' and students' technology use, we have not been able to capture a picture of what happens when technology is integrated into classrooms. As director of technology, I need to be able to answer this question.
>
> 2. Some teachers in our schools have not attained the level of technology integration that is desirable. They do not know how to integrate the use of technology with the cur-

riculum and learning opportunities in their classrooms.

Example 3: Patrick Kruchten. Patrick has been using portfolios with his students for years. His research grows out of his observations about why students struggle with the goal-setting process as it occurs in his classroom and from his desire to refine the current portfolio system to improve its effectiveness and to get students more involved in the process.

> I believe that students have goals, both academic and personal, that need to be met. Students have told me that we set "good goals," but that many times it's hard for them to work on a particular goal because I have set different priorities. I think that this places a lesser importance on student goals, and thus, I find it harder to have students work on them in school. By directly connecting student goals to our portfolios and our curriculum, I am hoping to help students be more motivated to act on the goals set.

Once teachers decide on a topic or general idea, they often read related literature, such as current articles in education journals or a recent study on a topic, and begin to formulate ideas about what actions to take. This reading often continues during the implementation and analysis stages.

Step 2: Describe the Actions and Articulate a Rationale

The researcher needs to decide on the specific actions to take and to study. This step in the process asks educators to clearly describe (1) the specific action(s) they will take; (2) a rationale for the action(s), including a discussion of the intended effects; (3) the people involved or affected by the actions; (4) the necessary resources needed to make the changes; and (5) any foreseeable prob-

lems or roadblocks that may come up, including confidentiality issues.

Example 1: Lisa Boerum. Lisa lists a series of actions that she plans on taking to tackle the challenges she will face. Her actions all relate to her goal of helping students to become observers of themselves, or researchers of their own learning. In addition to clearly describing her actions, she articulates a rationale for her plan.

ACTIONS
I will take the following actions with all of my 6th graders this year:

1. I will state my expectations for the year as follows: "Student will become a scientist/observer of self."
2. I will guide students in brainstorming qualities of learning. We will categorize and identify examples for these qualities.
3. I will guide students in picking areas to work on and help them to set goals.
4. Over the course of the year, during workshop days, I will include the following activities:
  • regular reflection
  • baseline reading/writing pieces
  • create/complete/collect work samples from homework and classwork
  • self-assessment using checklists to guide goal setting
  • goals, evidence, reflection, self/teacher assessments to be compiled quarterly for IEP (individualized education plan) portfolio

RATIONALE
One of the most important goals I have in working with my students is to make them more independent learners. In order to be independent, they need to develop an understanding of their strengths and weaknesses and of their disabilities. This self-knowledge is necessary if they are to set realistic and attainable goals for themselves. It is also necessary if they are to advocate for

themselves as they move from the middle school into the high school.

Example 2: Sue Cox. Sue chooses one specific action to tackle both problems she faces. She identifies her action, the formation of a collegial study group, and provides a rationale for her choice.

ACTION

I will establish a study group for teachers organized around the collaborative study of the question, "How can technology enhance learning?" I will study the changes in these teachers' use of technology and classroom practice as they engage in their own inquiry.

RATIONALE

Based on my own research, research by experts, seminars and symposiums, and my experience as a teacher and administrator, I believe a study group investigation of the impact of technology on teaching and learning will help teachers learn to choose technology effectively, focus on student learning, become reflective practitioners, and find time and support for their own professional growth. Further, I've learned that school-based activities are more likely to result in teachers' integrating of technology into the curriculum and instruction in their classrooms. I believe that active involvement, choice, and a learner-centered approach are important elements of learning for teachers as well as students. I also believe that active involvement in a technology-enhanced, learner-centered environment will prepare them to design this type of learning experience for students. Finally, I recognize the benefit of learning and working with a group of colleagues to improve my own practice and believe that participation in a collegial study group is a very powerful model of staff development.

Example 3: Patrick Kruchten. Patrick describes his actions related to improving his portfolio system and provides his rationale.

ACTIONS

I want to redesign my portfolio system so that it fully involves students in the process of setting goals and collecting artifacts to demonstrate progress on these goals on a regular basis. I will allow students to set goals for themselves, instead of the teacher and parent setting the goals, and directly connect their goals to the portfolios. I will change some of the use of time to allow for prioritizing of weekly goals, as well as searching for artifacts. I will also need to model how to set realistic goals, and the whole process of searching out specific artifacts that demonstrate specific learning. This will involve my current class of 27 students, 17 sixth graders and 10 fifth graders.

RATIONALE

I think that students will become much more invested in working on goals if they originate from them and they are responsible for collecting artifacts to prove progress. I also believe that students will be on task more, especially when they know that the work being completed could be an artifact to show goal progress. I also believe that goal setting and artifact collection will be a less arduous task when goals are directly related to portfolios and curriculum.

Step 3: Write Questions Related to the Actions

Action research questions are a vital part of planning. The questions(s) guide both the data collection and the analysis and reflection that will be done later. A specific research question (or questions) phrased so that the action is embedded will more effectively keep a researcher focused on studying his or her actions. In addition, research questions should not be yes/no questions. The phrasing should allow for analysis and reflection.

Example 1: Lisa Boerum. Lisa has a series of action research questions. Her first question is her "umbrella" question, the most important one. More specific questions under it relate to specific actions she is taking. Because the scope of her actions is wide, she has many questions that she can ask and pursue.

> In what ways will "personal investigation of learning" result in increased student self-expectations and performance levels?
>
> • How will goal setting increase student ownership of learning?
> • How will using a research framework with students clarify their sense of personal direction in learning?
> • How will reflection and self-assessments impact on students' ability to set self expectations, refine goals and actions, and communicate an understanding of their strengths and weaknesses more effectively?
> • How does the use of assessment checklists enable the student and teacher to refine and individualize the IEP and portfolio?

Example 2: Sue Cox. The teachers in Sue's study group are tackling the question, "How can technology enhance learning?" While they do so, Sue studies the impact of participation in the collegial study group.

> Question 1: How do teachers participating in this study group change the way they use technology in their classrooms?
> A. How do the study group teachers perceive the changes in their classrooms? How do they explain these changes?
> B. How does participation in the study group affect teachers' proficiency with technology?
> C. What impact does participation in the study group have on teachers' motivation to use technology?
> D. Does teachers' participation in the study group support teachers' willingness to risk investigating new technology uses and ex-

ploring ways to integrate them into curriculum and instruction? If so, what specific activities or aspects of the study group were most beneficial?

> Question 2: How has participation in the project affected teachers' classroom practice?
> A. Does the use of reflection in the study group affect these teachers' use of reflection in their classrooms?
> B. How does participation in a learner-centered study group affect the control of learning in their classrooms (teacher-centered or student-centered)?

Example 3: Patrick Kruchten. Patrick has two action research questions. The first is more broad and focuses on student learning, whereas the second is focused on using portfolios.

> 1. What impact is there on student learning when children are given ownership of portfolio design items such as goal setting, prioritization of learning, and artifact collection to demonstrate learning?
> 2. How will goal setting and collection of artifacts be affected when portfolio design is aligned with yearly goals?

Step 4: Plan for Data Collection

As the researcher begins to implement the actions decided upon, data collection also begins. The researcher needs to keep track of the specific actions taken, how they are taken, when, and how often. These are data related to the *actions*. The researcher also needs to collect data related to *results* of the actions. What happened that was expected? What happened that was unexpected?

Teachers may use a variety of strategies for data collection, including the following:

• anecdotal records
• audio-recordings/transcriptions
• checklists

- documents
- field notes
- journals/logs/diaries
- interviews
- photographs
- portfolios
- questionnaires/surveys
- schedules
- student work samples
- teacher work samples
- video-recordings

Example 1: Lisa Boerum. Here is how Lisa plans to collect data:

- Keep student portfolios with IEP plans.
- Keep monthly student reflections on goals and projects.
- Keep student assessment checklists.
- Save lesson plans related to goal setting, reflection, and use of checklists.

Example 2: Sue Cox. Here is how Sue plans to collect data:

- Take notes during and after study group meetings.
- Audio-tape each meeting and transcribe the tapes.
- Collect copies of individual teachers' research investigations and samples of their students' work.

Example 3: Patrick Kruchten. Here is how Patrick planned to collect data:

- Target a sample group of students to monitor closely.
- Keep copies of their portfolios, reflections, and goal setting.
- Keep a reflective journal/log to record observations and thoughts related to conferences, students, and portfolio work.
- Track my lessons related to goal setting and artifact collection.

Step 5: Create a Timetable

A timetable can be a helpful tool to guide action research. Sometimes educators resist taking the time to create one, but in the midst of teaching, caught up in the day-to-day crisis management of 27 1st graders or 140 high school juniors, a specific timetable can remind the researcher of the pieces of research that need attention.

Action researchers should be realistic and expect that they may need to modify the timetable as the project unfolds. The timetable should allow time for implementation, analysis and reflection, and revision of writing.

Example 1: Lisa Boerum. Lisa decides to collect data during the school year and save data analysis for the summer workshop days.

October–May	• Implement portfolios, monthly student reflection and goal setting, assessment checklists. • Collect data every month by duplicating students' reflections, goals, assessment checklists. • Keep lesson plans and notes related to lessons on portfolios, reflections, goals in binder.
June	• Duplicate portfolios from 12 students in 6th and 7th grade.
July–August	• Choose a subset of students. • Analyze data and draft response to research questions. • Prepare presentation to action researcher in the Center for the Study of Expertise in Teaching and Learning.

Example 2: Sue Cox. Sue decides to collect data and analyze it as she works. This makes sense given the nature of the study group and the fact that Sue is guiding the teachers through action research of their own.

September	• Send invitation to 20 teachers explaining purpose of study group and inviting them to join.
October–May	• Convene study group, tape meetings, take notes, collect samples of teacher and student work.
January–July	• Conduct ongoing data analysis.
July Institute	• Continue data analysis and draft response to research questions for professional portfolio.
September	• Send preliminary report to cohort 1 action researchers.

Example 3: Patrick Kruchten. Patrick creates a tentative plan for the year, fully expecting it to change as he begins to implement it. He writes a very detailed plan of what students, parents, and he will do. An excerpt is included here:

November 1998
Students will—
1. Brainstorm how we collect evidence and how to find artifacts to show progress.
2. Collect artifacts to show goals progress.
3. Present portfolios to parents.
4. Reflect on process collection and presentation.
5. Write a weekly reflection on work related to goals.
Parents will—
1. Reflect on process collection and presentation.
Teacher will—
1. Write a general reflection on how process went in class.
2. Lead a whole-group share of what is going well, not going well, record student responses.

What Roles Do Reading, Reflection, Analysis, and Writing Play?

Good classroom research builds upon prior experience, prior knowledge, and the work of others. As a researcher thinks about challenges, problems, or new approaches and decides on new actions or strategies to implement, it is natural to reflect on current practice and on the practice of others. Most teacher researchers read professional articles and books related to the new approaches and innovations they are trying in their classrooms. Often the work and experiences of others inform the initial decision making and the implementation of an action research project. In this way, reflection begins even in the early stages of an action research project.

Reflection continues as an educator implements new actions, strategies, and approaches and begins to collect data. It is natural for educators to look closely at what happens with students. As they implement new actions, they automatically look to see what works, what doesn't work, what the results are, what conditions affect the results, what might change, what might work better, and so on. And so, reflection is happening before teachers or administrators are really "finished" with the work. For these reasons, it is a good idea for researchers to document their thinking as they proceed—to tape-record it or write it down so that when they come to the final stage of data analysis and reflection, they will have their earlier reflections to go back to.

The real learning in this entire process comes when a teacher or an administrator closely examines the data that has been collected to make sense of it. As researchers attempt to answer their questions, they learn about the efficacy of their actions, the limitations, the possibilities. Finally, the act of writing to communicate the learning forces them to think more clearly and therefore to really understand what their research is telling them.

What Are the Criteria for a Quality Plan?

As educators get ready to do action research, it is important that they take the time to carefully think through their plan. Appendix E contains a

Checklist for Quality and a Rubric for an Action Research Plan. These tools can help action researchers assess the quality of their plans before implementing a project. In particular, the checklist and the rubric can allow researchers to adjust and revise a plan so that it is more clear and specific.

What Does Data Analysis Look Like?

Some researchers plan action research so that they collect data for a period of time and then systematically review and analyze that data after implementation. Lisa Boerum's approach illustrates this. She chose to do data analysis after the school year was over simply because she didn't have time to do it during the school year, given the professional demands she faces. Others start the review and analysis while the implementation and collection are still going on. For Sue Cox, the ongoing analysis allowed her to better lead the collegial study group of teacher researchers and make thoughtful adjustments to the process.

Often teachers ask, "How do I begin to analyze data?" The answer relates directly back to the questions posed in the action research study. Some studies require more quantitative analysis and others require more qualitative analysis, but most require both. To conduct quantitative analysis, the researcher should be comfortable with numbers and statistics. The process of data analysis in a quantitative study is more numerical, clear, and straightforward. This kind of data analysis may be one of the reasons why some educators hesitate to consider action research. However, when several teachers work together, they can pool their skills. Sometimes a school district will pay a math teacher or university professor to help. Many action research

studies do not require statistical analysis, or the analysis is relatively modest and easily managed by teachers with some background in mathematics.

The three examples in this chapter involve both qualitative and quantitative data analysis. This joint analysis requires much sifting, sorting, close reading, and decision making. Sometimes the researcher needs to look for patterns, emerging themes or questions, inconsistencies, or paradoxes in the data. Sometimes the data analysis involves categorizing responses and tallying types of responses. At other times it involves comparing pre- and post-measures or noting the frequency of a behavior or response.

The following example of data analysis by Patrick Kruchten shows how he went about analyzing student responses. This particular analysis required no extraordinary mathematical skills. Patrick simply had to categorize and tally types of responses for this part of his data analysis.

> As I read each student response, I made notes in the margins about what the response was about. I then grouped the responses into categories and tallied the number in each category. For question 1, I found the following information:
>
> Question 1: What do you really like about portfolios?
> - 10 responses that they liked organization
> - 11 responses that they liked how their portfolio showed evidence of learning
> - 4 responses that their description of their artifacts were detailed
> - 1 response that he/she liked how the portfolio showed growth
> - 1 response that he/she liked how the portfolio compared old work to new work

Whether the analysis is qualitative or quantitative, the researcher needs to be systematic in coding and organizing the data. Otherwise, the researcher risks drawing conclusions based on impressions or perceptions. The more systematic the approach to data analysis, the less overwhelmed a researcher will become by the amount of data to sift through.

What Forums Allow Educators to Share Their Action Research?

When educators share their action research with others, they learn more from it, and they allow others to learn. The process of articulating research and letting others know what has been discovered helps researchers to make meaning from their work. Educators can use many forums to share their research. These include collegial groups, portfolios, newsletters, articles in professional journals, and presentations at professional conferences, symposiums, and district or department meetings.

Recommended Resources

Bissex, G. L., & Bullock, R. H. (Eds.). (1987). *Seeing for ourselves: Case study research by teachers of writing.* Portsmouth, NH: Heinemann.
This book is a collection of case studies by teachers of English and graduate students. These studies demonstrate the value of classroom-based research and argue that teacher research does not have to involved large numbers of subjects, control groups, and statistics to be valuable.

Burnaford, G., Fischer, J., & Hobsen, D. (1996). *Teachers doing research: Practical possibilities.* Mahwah, NJ: Lawrence Erlbaum Associates.
This collection of articles about teacher research has sections for beginners as well as for those already informed about teacher research. The focus is practical, and the book includes suggestions for how to do research and how to build a learning community of teach-

ers supporting each other. The authors share a variety of teacher research projects.

Glanz, J. (1998). *Action research: An educational leader's guide to school improvement.* Norwood, MA: Christopher-Gordon Publishers.
This book provides the reader with background on educational research and discusses a variety of ways to use action research in an educational setting. The purpose of action research, as described, is to guide decision making and planning. The material is thorough and easy to read and includes helpful examples. The steps necessary for carrying out action research are reviewed in a user-friendly fashion. The book could serve as a text or study group resource. Exercises and prompts throughout help the reader reflect on the information and strategies and think about application of the models described. The program and evaluation chapter details steps to follow when implementing new programs or evaluating existing programs. The author discusses in detail the reality of day-to-day decisions, deadlines for decisions that come too quickly, and the need for a better model. Although the text would be helpful to individuals who want to use action research, it would be best used with a committee or a study group. The book's readability and its strategies for action research in a meaningful context make it a valuable resource and reference.

Kemmis, S., & Taggart, R. (Eds.). (1988). *The action research planner* (3rd ed.). Geelong, Victoria, Australia: Deakin University Press.
This book clearly describes stages of action research and offers guidelines for developing and implementing an action research project. Emphasis is placed on the recursive nature of the process and on the need for reflection.

Noffke, S. E., & Stevenson, R. B. (1995). *Educational action research: Becoming practically critical.* NY: Teachers College Press.
This collection of essays offers a multitude of perspectives on action research. Its detail and diversity, tapping into the experiences of teachers, student teachers, staff developers, principals, and others, makes for thought-provoking reading. The authors focus on the value of action research as part of school improvement. Divided into three main parts, "Action Research in Teacher Education," "Action Research in Schools," and "Supporting Action Research," this book invites readers to examine the potential, the problems, and the impact of action research in education.

Embracing It All

9

> **Essential Question:**
> **What Does It Look Like to Be a**
> **Learner-Centered Teacher?**

This chapter is about putting the pieces together. It tackles the question, What does it look like to do this? Perhaps the most important issue to consider here is that embracing the eight innovations discussed in the previous chapters is more about beliefs than about techniques. Some of these beliefs concern teachers themselves, and others relate to their work. Some of these beliefs run contrary to common teaching practices, such as the belief that teachers are responsible for designing and not just implementing curriculum. The most important belief related to teachers' work is that attention should be placed on students' learning and not on what should be taught. The most critical belief related to individuals themselves is that changing and improving is a journey and not a series of events. In short, teachers need to see themselves as professionals.

Many schools do not operate in ways that support these beliefs. Textbooks and state mandates drive too much of what is taught. Administrators and boards of education seldom provide teachers with the necessary time to develop their own curriculum or to adapt textbooks and translate state mandates in ways that are respectful of a specific group of students or community. The pressure to help students pass tests or meet state standards prevents many teachers from focusing on student learning instead of "covering" the curriculum. Finally, the reality of facing a specific group of students on a regular basis makes it difficult for teachers to assume a long-term view toward design. Instead, teachers want to develop or use something tomorrow—if not today. It is difficult for educators to be patient with themselves when they know that the time they have with a particular group of students is ephemeral.

Even though all the innovations described in this book support a learner-centered classroom, teachers do not need to implement them all at the same time. Instead, they can select innovations on the basis of how well they match their own belief system, their access to resources, their working environment, and other constraints posed by their supervisors or programs. Following are possible beginning steps for each of the innovations presented in this book.

Essential Questions

To begin using essential questions, teachers can identify one or two essential questions for the year and use them to make connections among different units of study. For example, the question, Who am I? can be used at the kindergarten level as the connecting thread among units having to do with children's bodies, families, and backgrounds. The question, Does conflict support social change? can be used to link units on different historical periods and events. What is art? can be used to ponder the meaning and manifestations of art across time and places.

A different beginning point is to identify a unit or theme that lends itself to student inquiry—that is, a unit in which the students can be in charge of investigating something in depth. For this kind of unit, teachers can use an essential question and supporting guiding questions as the springboard for the unit and as a pre- and post-test of what was learned. For example, a group of middle school teachers are using the question, What would it take for the world to feed itself? to launch a middle school unit on hunger. The students will engage in a series of experiences exploring the causes of, manifestations of, and alternatives to world hunger.

Integrated Curriculum

One of the first steps in using an integrated curriculum involves carefully mapping and examining the curriculum taught over the course of the year to find natural connections that teachers may have overlooked. Such maps are often chronological and include the specific curriculum components that teachers consider important. Some teachers organize their curriculum in terms of units, whereas others think in terms of texts or readings. Some teachers teach conceptually, whereas others perceive what they teach in terms of specific skills and strategies. Figure 9.1 is an example of a possible mapping structure. Teachers can map individually or with other teachers to look for better ways of integrating what they do, or to find gaps and redundancies in their curriculum.

Another starting point in the use of integrated curriculum is to transform an existing topic-based unit (for example, the American Revolution, or My Neighborhood) into a conceptual or issue-based unit such as War or Community. For example, if teachers used the concept of Community instead of the theme of My Neighborhood, they could ask students to identify the elements of all communities and not just of their neighborhood. The class could also explore different kinds of communities, including those in which various students have lived. This transformation would foster students' conceptual understanding while supporting natural connections between subjects and content areas (social studies, science, language arts), and between the students' own background knowledge and the material included in the unit.

FIGURE 9.1
A MAPPING STRUCTURE FOR PLANNING AN INTEGRATED CURRICULUM

Month	Unit/theme	Skills	Materials/resources used	Assessments
September				
October				
November				

Standards-Based Curriculum and Assessment Design

Standards-based design can begin with at least two different approaches. One of them involves becoming familiar with existing school, state, or national standards and analyzing them to determine the existing relationship between what the teacher does and what the teacher should be doing. This is often known as a gap analysis process. Like curriculum mapping, it involves identifying different aspects of the curriculum; but unlike mapping, it requires that such identification be done against standards and benchmarks or indicators. Figure 9.2 shows a sample structure for doing a gap analysis for language arts standards and includes an example of a completed entry.

A second approach to beginning standards-based design involves teachers generating their own exit outcomes and indicators, and answering these questions: What do I want my students to know, be able to do, or value by the end of the year? and What do each of these outcomes look like in terms of students' behaviors or activities? Having generated this list, a teacher can then examine its relationship to the textbook or curriculum. Such analysis should result in teaching more strategically to specific outcomes and in the development of priorities for delivering an ever-growing body of content.

Authentic Assessment

One way that teachers can begin to use authentic assessment is to look at all the projects and performances that students might engage in during the year and reconfigure as many as possible so that they incorporate authentic assessment attributes. The most important of these attributes is the use of real-life problems and challenges in a presentation or demonstration for audiences who can benefit from the information or skills gained. For example, the three book reports a teacher usually assigns could become a book review for a children's magazine, a poster for a book fair, and a persuasive letter to the school librarian recommending the book for purchase. The traditional research report can become an editorial on why society should support or ban a specific technology. The oral presentation can become an interactive how-to lesson delivered by one group of students to another group of students.

Another way to begin using authentic assessment involves reconfiguring a specific unit that is fundamentally information-based to make it more focused on authentic application. In this unit, students would grapple with and conduct research on a real problem or issue, such as the media's manipulation of people's self-image, and develop a performance or a product to address this problem and perhaps teach others about it.

Rubrics

Rubrics go hand-in-hand with authentic assessment, but teachers do not need to develop a rubric to begin to appreciate the merits of one. For example, whenever teachers introduce any genre, they can use real-world exemplars or models and ask students: What makes this good? At another time they can show students two or three examples of defective or unsophisticated work related to the same genre and ask students: What is missing here? or Why is this sample not as good as the exemplars we reviewed before? This exercise with contrasting work generates different lists of quality indicators that teachers can use to focus their instruction or that the students can use to guide themselves in producing their own work.

FIGURE 9.2
A GAP ANALYSIS FOR LANGUAGE ARTS STANDARDS

Benchmark/ indicator	What I do in the classroom	How I teach this	What I do to assess students' learning	The level of students' mastery that I work toward
Interpret and analyze information from different kinds of texts.	Interpret graphs and charts (immigration unit)	Homework assignment (2 graphs and 2 charts)	Checklist and note cards	Reinforcement
Compare and synthesize information from different sources.				
Distinguish between facts and opinions in different sources.				

Alternatively, throughout the year, teachers can systematically collect a few samples of students' work that represent three or four different levels of quality for complex assignments or for assignments that, in the past, have resulted in significantly varying qualities of work. These work samples can be "cleaned" so that the students who produced them cannot be identified and be placed in folders labeled with the name of the assignment. Teachers can use these samples when they introduce a new group of students to the same kinds of assignments. This introduction is most effective when teachers give students a random set of samples and ask them to sort them into three or four piles representing different levels of quality work and to describe the characteristics of each pile.

Portfolios

One way to begin the use of portfolios is to identify a specific aspect of student learning for which documenting growth is essential, or for which having students select and reflect on work over time would be most beneficial. This area of focus may be a skill, such as problem solving, or an outcome or standard, such as writing for a variety of purposes and audiences or using geographic knowledge and skills to understand the world in which we live. What is important is that students are guided through the selection, reflection, and evaluation of this work so that it becomes a meaningful learning experience as well as an assessment tool. Such guidance involves modeling the process as well as giving students prompts that can help them choose and evaluate the work. It also requires that teachers give students feedback on their portfolios, not in terms of agreeing or disagreeing with the choices students have made, but rather in terms of letting

them know what such choices and reflections reveal to a reader of their work.

Another starting point with portfolios involves teachers developing their own purposeful work collections. Such collections could be of curriculum and assessment work-in-progress, of work that depicts the different aspects of teaching or the profession, or of work that shows the teacher as a lifelong learner. Teachers can use their portfolios to introduce students to the concept of portfolio assessment or as vehicles to legitimize their professionalism as they look for a different job or seek new professional opportunities.

Reflection

Introducing reflection into teaching is easy if teachers embrace the conviction that it is important for students and educators to be thoughtful. The focus of reflection can be learning, teaching, work, or thinking. It is easy to imagine a classroom where no reflection is fostered. It is a classroom where students are always passively listening to a teacher or taking notes, or where students are continually practicing isolated skills or completing worksheets. It is harder to imagine a class with too much reflection, although reflection prompts can be overused if they become "canned" questions that teachers ask students at the end of each activity or project.

To begin to cultivate reflection, teachers should look for natural opportunities when learning about students' thinking would be of benefit. For example, when students are introduced to group work and engage in their first cooperative learning activity, a teacher may ask the students questions such as these: What were you able to do as a group? How did you resolve your differences of opinion?

What got in the way of the group's ability to do the task? What helped the group move forward? What could we do differently next time so that the groups function better than they did before?

Action Research

The cultivation of action research can begin in several ways. One way involves identifying an area or issue that a teacher is genuinely unsure about and gathering information on how others view or engage with the same issue. An alternative is to identify the same issue or question but gather information on how the teacher approaches the issue in different settings or with different students. The key ingredient in either case is to gather and study the information systematically so that the teacher can better understand the problem and make adjustments in practice based on that learning. Action research can also be cultivated when teachers work collaboratively to study and discuss a problem they all share or an issue they are all interested in.

Clearly, there are as many starting points for adopting the innovations presented in this book as there are individual preferences. What is important is that teachers embrace the innovations as evolving learning experiences rather than as discrete techniques to be mastered, and that they see learning as a journey toward becoming true learners of their own profession.

Appendix A: Tools for Developing a Curriculum Unit

Curriculum Unit Design Module

Organizing Center
Identify your organizing center. This is the concept, issue, theme, or topic that holds the unit together.

Preliminary Rationale
Describe, as best as you can, why you have selected this center. What will a unit focused on this organizing center do for students? For you?

Essential Questions
Generate one or more essential questions for the unit.

Guiding Questions
For each essential question, identify one or more guiding questions (objectives turned into answer-able questions). For example, a guiding question for the essential question "Should all citizens be treated equally?" may be "What are the rights of federal prisoners?"

Rationale for Unit
Describe why this unit should be taught. Refer to the preliminary rationale you wrote. What justifies the time and energy you and your students will invest? What will students demonstrate that they know and are able to do?

Context or Overview
Write a brief description of where this unit will fit within the overall curriculum. Is the unit subject-centered or interdisciplinary? What knowledge, skills, or dispositions will you teach before teaching this unit? Who is the unit for? When will you teach it? How long will you teach it for?

Culminating Authentic Assessment Task
Describe the authentic assessment(s) for your unit.

Authenticity of the Culminating Assessment
Assess the authenticity of your culminating assessment by answering the following questions:

- Does it require students to deal with a real problem or issue?
- Does it provide students with a real purpose for engaging in the task?
- Are there real consequences for the success or failure of the task (other than receiving credit or a grade)?
- Does it provide students with a real audience that could benefit or learn something from the task?

If you answered no to any of the preceding questions, revise your task accordingly.

Authentic Assessment(s) Revision
If necessary, revise your authentic assessment(s).

Place your authentic assessment in the Unit Sketch (see p. 109).

Diagnostic and Formative Assessment Opportunities
Describe diagnostic and/or formative assessments connected to the unit. Place them in the Unit Sketch.

Exit Outcomes—Knowledge
What will students know about? Identify the knowledge students will acquire. Focus on general concepts and ideas (e.g., basic rights and responsibilities) rather than on isolated facts (e.g., date when women were allowed to vote).

Exit Outcomes—Skills
What should students be able to do? Describe the skills that your students will acquire and demonstrate.

Exit Outcomes—Thinking Skills
What thinking skills should students use and demonstrate?

Exit Outcomes—Values
What should students value? Identify the attitudes, perceptions, and dispositions that your unit will foster (e.g., respect for cultural differences, tolerance for differing opinions, appreciation of literature).

National Standards and Benchmark
List the standards and benchmark that will be measured by the assessments in your unit.

District and State Standards
Review and identify the district and state standards that are most closely related to your unit and that will be measured by the assessments. Write down the specific standards and indicators you will be directly addressing.

Learning Opportunities/Lessons
Describe the learning opportunities and lessons that will support student success on the unit. Sketch the lessons.

Criteria for Performance
List the criteria that will form the basis of checklists/rubrics you will use to assess the product(s) or performance(s) in the culminating assessment task. The list should include the performance indicators you have selected for the national and state standards you identified.

Reflective Prompts
Write the reflective questions or prompts you will use to help students think about their learning. Place them in your unit sketch.

Template for a Unit Sketch

	Monday	Tuesday	Wednesday	Thursday	Friday
Week 1					
Week 2					
Week 3					
Week 4					

A Rubric for Developing a Curriculum Unit

Dimension	n/s*	1	2	3	4
Unit Structure and Clarity		• Some but not all unit components are included. • Description of components is incomplete or ambiguous. • Unit sketch is missing or indecipherable • Unit includes no student work, or student work detracts from the unit. It is difficult to tell what the student work relates to.	• All unit components are included. • Unit alludes to most important foundational knowledge, skills, and logistical components. • Unit sketch is incomplete. • Student work for most salient unit components is included. • Student work is related to a single aspect of student achievement.	• Components are well organized and sequential. • A description of foundational knowledge, skills, and logistical requirements is included. • Unit sketch lays out the unit components sequentially. • Student work that is included illustrates selected unit components. • Student work illustrates multiple aspects of growth or achievement.	• Components are carefully thought out and strategically designed. • A comprehensive description and illustration of all foundational knowledge, skills, and logistical requirements is included. • Unit sketch is clear and comprehensive and shows how each component supports coherence. • Selected student work illustrates and enhances all aspects of the unit. • Student work depicts how the unit supports student growth and achievement for different kinds of learners.
Unit Description and Focus		• States grade level, subject, and title of unit. • Lists theme, concept, issue, or problem addressed. • Is incomplete and lacks focus.	• Identifies title, grade level, subject, and demands of the unit. • Briefly describes the theme, concept, issue, or problem addressed.	• Provides clear information about grade level, subject, and demands of the unit. • Describes and justifies the theme, concept, issue, or problem addressed.	• Includes extensive information about grade level, subject, time and resource demands imposed by the unit. • Clearly, concisely, and thoroughly

*n/s = Not scorable given the information included.

	• describes and justifies the theme, concept, issue, or problem addressed. • Shows how each of the unit components is supported and driven by the central theme, concept, issue, or problem.	• Is focused and developed but does not provide a full picture of how the unit components address the central theme, concept, issue, or problem.	• Is focused but not fully developed.	
Rationale	• Eloquent and substantive; no one would doubt that this unit is important. • Addresses the specific knowledge, skills, and dispositions students will acquire.	• Clear and relevant in terms of justifying content and skills.	• Developed and clear but superficial.	• Unclear or trivial. Not sufficiently developed.
Alignment with District, State, and/or National Standards	• Alignment with standards is clear and explicit throughout the unit. • Learning opportunities and assessments are directly related and clearly support students' attainment of the standards.	• Alignment with standards is clear and explicit but is not embedded in the learning opportunities for students. • Learning opportunities and assessments are directly related to the standards.	• Alignment with standards is not explicit but can be inferred. • Learning opportunities and assessments are partially related to the standards.	• Alignment is contrived or difficult to determine. • Learning opportunities and assessments appear to be unrelated to the standards.
Essential and Guiding Questions	• Questions are compelling. • Questions provide the central focus	• Questions are significant, open-ended, and clearly stated.	• Questions are clear and open-ended but not significant.	• Questions are missing, unclear, or poorly stated.

(continues on next page)

A Rubric for Developing a Curriculum Unit *(continued)*

Dimension	n/s*	1	2	3	4
Essential and Guiding Questions—*(continued)*		• Questions are irrelevant to inquiry. • Questions are divorced from the unit content. • Unit relies exclusively on guiding questions.	• Questions support inquiry. • Questions relate to the unit's content. • Guiding questions relate to the essential question.	• Questions foster understanding and inquiry. • Questions are intrinsically tied to the unit content. • Guiding questions support the essential question.	that drives students' inquiry. • Questions are addressed throughout the unit and clearly support students' attainment of standards. • Unit is supported by guiding questions that provide meaningful access to the essential question.
Levels of Thinking		• Focuses exclusively on recall, comprehension, and basic application of knowledge and skills.	• Focuses primarily on recall, comprehension, and factual knowledge acquisition. • Includes one or more questions or activities that require higher-order thinking.	• Addresses all levels of thinking, moving from basic to higher-order thinking.	• Integrates the use of basic and higher levels of thinking supporting the meaningful construction of knowledge.
Learning Styles/ Multiple Intelligences		• Is geared toward a single learning style/intelligence.	• Learning opportunities provide for a limited range of learning styles/intelligences. • Assessment supports a single style of learning.	• Learning opportunities and assessments support several learning styles/intelligences.	• Learning opportunities and assessments allow students to draw upon their preferred learning style/intelligence.

Types of Learning Environments	• Relies on a single form/structure for learning (i.e., cooperative, individual, or competitive learning).	• Addresses two or more types of learning that are unconnected from each other.	• Students learn individually and in groups, although the learning from each of these forms is not maximized.	• Maximizes the use of individual, cooperative, and competitive learning. • Encourages individual as well as group accountability and interdependence.
Academic Rigor and Supporting Resources	• Aims at enabling students to recall isolated concepts, skills, and/or facts. • Resources are incomplete, questionable, and superficially related to the unit's focus. • Relies exclusively on students' experience and knowledge or on inappropriate resources.	• Enables students to develop a rudimentary background on a concept, problem, and/or skills. • Resources are relevant but limited in scope and depth. • Overly reliant on one kind of resource.	• Enables students to develop an understanding and use of knowledge and skills acquired related to a theme, problem, issue. • Resources are substantive and varied in form and focus. • Resources are directly related to the unit's focus.	• Requires students to engage in a thorough exploration of a theme, problem, issue, or question by emulating professionals in the area in question. • Resources are substantive, up-to-date, and span a wide range of forms and media. • Resources directly support the unit by fostering an exploration of multiple perspectives related to the unit's focus.
Forms and Quality of Integration	• Requires students to acquire knowledge and skills within a single content area. • Is presented in ways that prevent students from making meaningful connections between their experiences and the unit material.	• Requires students to use knowledge and skills from two content areas not naturally related to one another. • Forces contrived connections between students' own experiences and the material presented.	• Requires students to use knowledge and skills in ways that integrate naturally related subject areas. • Allows students to derive personal meaning from the material presented.	• Requires students to use and integrate knowledge and skills from a variety of naturally related areas in ways that enhance each content area.

(continues on next page)

A Rubric for Developing a Curriculum Unit *(continued)*

Dimension	n/s*	1	2	3	4
Forms and Quality of Integration— *(continued)*					• Explicitly draws on students' interests, backgrounds, cultures, and experiences as a foundation for its study.
Authenticity and Congruence of the Curriculum and Assessments		• Learning opportunities and assessments are contrived and divorced from real-life problems and audiences. • Assessments are unrelated to the unit.	• Learning opportunities involve students in a combination of contrived and plausible problems/tasks. • Assessments do not address learning from tasks and are appended to the curriculum. • Only some aspects of the curriculum are measured.	• Learning opportunities involve students in plausible or realistic problems/tasks. • Assessments do not fully address learning from tasks. • Assessment is linked to the curriculum in ways that support and measure student learning. • It is clear where the curriculum ends and the assessment begins.	• Unit requires that students engage in real-life problems and demonstrate such learning to audiences that could benefit from that demonstration. • Assessment is derived from curriculum-embedded learning opportunities that measure and enhance student learning. • Curriculum and assessment activities are so intertwined that it is difficult to tell where curriculum ends and assessment begins.

Timing, Nature, and Flexibility of Assessments				
	• Formal assessment is limited to end-of-unit activities • Unit time is fixed, with no choice of what or how to learn.	• Includes diagnostic as well as summative (end-of-unit) assessments. • Diagnostic assessment is not used as a supplement or support for the summative evaluation. • What to learn and how to show learning are predetermined by teacher, with limited student choice. • Unit has fixed time constraints.	• Includes discrete diagnostic, formative, and summative assessments. • Students can select from a wide range of teacher-predetermined choices for what to learn or how to demonstrate learning. • Time allotted to learn and demonstrate learning is fixed.	• Is formally assessed from beginning to end to measure and support student learning and to inform teaching. • Allows for a wide range of teacher- and student-negotiated choice of what to learn and, where appropriate, how to demonstrate learning. • Time allotted to learn and demonstrate learning is individualized and linked to the different assessment demands.

Source: Center for the Study of Expertise in Teaching and Learning (CSETL) (1998). Copyright 1998 by CSETL. Used by permission.

Curriculum Unit Ratings

Title of Unit: _____

Dimensions	Ratings (1–4)
• Unit Structure and Clarity • Unit Description and Focus • Rationale • Alignment with Standards • Essential and Guiding Questions • Levels of Thinking • Learning Styles/Multiple Intelligences • Types of Learning Environments • Academic Rigor and Supporting Resources • Forms and Quality of Integration • Authenticity of Congruence of the Curriculum and Assessments • Timing, Nature, and Flexibility of Assessments	

Source: Center for the Study of Expertise in Teaching and Learning (CSETL) (1998). Copyright 1998 by CSETL. Used by permission.

Appendix B: Tools for Developing Authentic Assessments

Authentic Assessment Design Module

Context for Authentic Assessment
Describe what comes before; prior experiences of students; where the task/project fits in the curriculum.

Authentic Assessment(s)
Describe the authentic assessment(s).

Standards and Indicators
List the standards and indicators that are assessed by the assessment.

Learning Opportunities/Lessons
Describe the lessons and/or learning opportunities that will support student success on the assessment.

Assessment Opportunities
Describe the diagnostic and/or formative assessments connected to the authentic assessment.

Performance Criteria
Describe the criteria you will be using to score or grade the assessment. The standard indicators you have identified should serve as the basis for your criteria.

Use the rubric template on page 118 to develop the scoring rubric for your task based on the preceding performance criteria. (See Chapter 5 for assistance.)

Rubric Template

Dimension	4	3	2	1

Rubric for Authentic Classroom Assessment Tasks

Dimension	n/s*	1	2	3	4
Real Audience and Purpose		• Teacher is the only audience. • Purpose is to measure/test. • Assessment has no real consequences beyond getting credit or a grade. • Assessment is contrived and has little connection with reality outside of school. • Assessment requires students to engage with isolated skills or facts.	• Audience consists of teachers and peers. • Purpose is vague or only school-related. • Assessment has no real consequences beyond the classroom. • Assessment is derived from a plausible situation and resembles some aspects of reality outside of school. • Assessment requires students to engage with part of a problem/situation.	• Audience consists of teachers, peers, and/or parents. • Assessment has a real purpose. • Assessment could have real consequences for students if it had an audience that could use or benefit from this work. • Is derived from a plausible situation that could be real with minor changes. • Requires students to engage with a complex situation or issue.	• Assessment has a real and invested audience beyond the classroom or a classroom/school audience that has a stake in learning. • Assessment has a real and meaningful purpose. • Students experience the benefits and consequences of their work. • Assessment is derived from a real need, problem, or issue in need of attention. • Assessment requires students to engage with a real situation or issue.
Integration of Subjects/Content Areas		• Measures students' ability to use a specific skill in a specific content area.	• Requires students to build upon prior knowledge from two or more content areas that are not intrinsically related to the task's purpose.	• Requires students to build upon prior knowledge. • Requires students to apply knowledge and skills from two or more content areas that support the task.	• Requires students to use prior knowledge in a meaningful way. • Requires students to apply knowledge and skills from two or more naturally related content areas that enhance each one.

(continues on next page)

*n/s = Not scorable given the information included.

Rubric for Authentic Classroom Assessment Tasks *(continued)*

Dimension	n/s*	1	2	3	4
Disciplined Inquiry/ Academic Rigor		• Requires no research on the part of the student.	• Requires students to engage in limited research focused on finding specific and discrete information predetermined by the teacher.	• Requires that students explore different aspects of an issue or topic through research. • Research draws on selected sources and relies on limited strategies.	• Requires that students search for in-depth understanding through systematic research and inquiry. • Students use a variety of primary and secondary sources. • Students use a variety of research strategies, such as oral interviews, surveys, computer searches.
Elaborate Communication		• Requires minimal response. • Is limited to answers to multiple-choice, true-false questions, or yes/no responses.	• Requires some verbal/written communication. • Is limited to short test answers or question-based oral responses.	• Requires communication of knowledge and/or skills through written, artistic, and/or oral performances.	• Requires elaborate communication of knowledge, skills, and process through written, artistic, oral performances, exhibitions, and/or opportunities for students to teach others.
Explicit Standards and Scoring Criteria		• The task lacks specific performance standards. • Teacher's criteria are unknown to the students. • The task is presented by itself;	• Performance standards for the task have been partially identified in checklists that identify criteria but do not distinguish among	• Performance standards for the task are identified and articulated in rubrics that effectively distinguish various levels of performance.	• Performance standards for the task were jointly identified and articulated by both teacher and students in rubrics that effectively dis-

	tinguish levels of performance. • Criteria guide students in evaluation and goal setting. • A variety of exemplars and anchors illustrate the different levels of performance.	• Criteria are clear. • A variety of exemplars illustrate quality work.	levels of performance. • Criteria are vague. • Includes one or two models that illustrate quality work.	there are no models that illustrate quality work.
Flexibility in Content, Strategies, Products, and Time	• Assessment allows student-generated choice of content or strategies. • Time allotment is flexible for different students and accommodates differences among the products/performances selected.	• Students have a wide variety of teacher-generated choices of content, strategies, or products. • Time allotment is flexible for different students but is not tied to the actual task demands.	• Students have limited choice of content (they must choose from a list of topics). • Strategies or products are the same for everyone; time may be flexible in terms of content or strategies, but it is fixed with regard to the deadline for the product.	• All students work with the same material, use the same strategies, and develop the same product. • Time and deadlines are fixed.
Diagnostic, Formative, and Summative Assessment	• Lesson/unit is formally assessed from beginning to end to measure and support student learning and to inform teaching via a variety of diagnostic, formative, and summative assessments.	• Includes discrete diagnostic, formative, and summative assessments that relate to one another.	• Includes diagnostic as well as summative assessment. • Diagnostic assessment is not used as a supplement or support for the summative evaluation.	• Relies only on summative or end-of-lesson/unit assessment.

(continues on next page)

Rubric for Authentic Classroom Assessment Tasks (*continued*)

Dimension	n/s*	1	2	3	4
Metacognition, Self-Assessment, Peer Assessment, and Feedback		• Teacher is the only person who reflects on the products and processes. • There are no reflection questions, checklists, or rubrics. • Teacher is the sole evaluator. • Feedback is very general and given only after the task is completed.	• Students reflect in general. • Reflection questions, checklists, or rubrics are only peripherally related to the assessment. • Students evaluate their own products. • Feedback is specific but given only after the task is completed. • Revision is allowed but not encouraged.	• Students reflect on the final product. • Reflection takes the form of specific questions, checklists, or rubrics. • Peers give feedback on each other's work during different phases of the task. • Feedback is specific throughout and encourages students to revise.	• Students reflect on both products and processes. • Reflection takes the form of ongoing and specific questions, checklists, or rubrics. • Students formally evaluate their own and each other's tasks throughout the assessment experience. • Feedback is elaborate and specific and comes from both the teacher and peers. • Feedback encourages revision to produce quality work.
Levels of Thinking		• Assessment focuses exclusively on recall, comprehension, and basic application of knowledge and skills.	• Assessment focuses primarily on recall, comprehension, and acquisition of facts although it includes one or more questions or activities that require higher-order thinking.	• Assessment addresses all levels of thinking, moving from basic to higher-order thinking.	• Assessment integrates the use of basic and higher levels of thinking. • Task naturally calls for a combination of skills and forms of knowledge.

Source: Center for the Study of Expertise in Teaching and Learning (CSETL) (1998). Copyright 1998 by CSETL. Used by permission.

Assessment Ratings

Title of Assessment: _____

Dimensions	Ratings (1–4)
• Real Audience and Purpose • Integration of Subjects/Content Areas • Disciplined Inquiry/Academic Rigor • Elaborate Communication • Explicit Standards and Scoring Criteria • Flexibility in Content, Strategies, Products, and Time • Use of Diagnostic, Formative, and Summative Assessment • Metacognition, Self-Assessment, Peer Assessment, and Feedback • Levels of Thinking	

Source: Center for the Study of Expertise in Teaching and Learning (CSETL) (1998). Copyright 1998 by CSETL. Used by permission.

Appendix C: Tools for Designing Portfolio Assessments

Questions to Guide the Portfolio Design Process

What is the primary purpose of the portfolio your students will keep? Who is the primary audience? Secondary audience?

What will the portfolio document? (A portfolio may document growth, achievement, effort, or combinations of these toward standards or understanding of curriculum content.)

What is the portfolio's focus? What are the standards it is connected to? What parts of the curriculum is it connected to?

What possible things could students put into a portfolio that connect to these standards and cur-

riculum? Identify possible portfolio contents. Link contents to the standards and curriculum.

What is the time line for the collection of student work?

How and when will you introduce the portfolio to students? How will you teach them what it is about?

How and when will students reflect and select entries? How often? At what time of the day? With what kind of assistance or guidance?

How will you inform parents about the portfolio their children are keeping? Will students share their portfolios with their parents? If so, how?

What management system will you use to help you and your students save work so that they can review, reflect, and select? How will you and your students file and save selections (folders, binders, file drawers, boxes, large envelopes, pizza boxes)?

How will you ask or guide students to select entries? Write specific instructions you will give them.

How will you ask students to reflect on what they select? What questions will you ask them to help them to reflect on their selections?

What specific strategies will you use to teach students about quality reflection? What lessons will you teach?

Portfolio Entries or Requirements

September

October

November

December

January

February

March

April

May

June

Appendix D: Reflection Prompts and Questions

Reflection prompts and questions can be written from the student's point of view ("I chose this essay because . . .") or from the teacher's point of view ("What did you like best about this essay?). Choose whichever approach seems most suited to the situation.

Reflection Prompts for Lessons

- One thing that I learned today was _____.
- One thing that surprised me today was

    _____.

- If I had taught this lesson myself, I would have _____.

Reflection Prompts, Questions, and Checklists for Individual Pieces of Work

- Why did I select this particular essay (or sample of writing)?

- What are its special strengths?
- What have I learned about writing from working on this essay (writing sample)?
- If I could do this essay (writing) over what I would do is _____.

- Why did you select this particular piece?
- What do you see as the special strengths of this work? What do you think your readers, viewers, etc., already know about what you say?
- What do you think you have to tell them?
- How do you expect this piece of writing to affect your readers?
- What have you learned about reading, writing, etc., from your work on this piece?
- If you could go on working on this piece, what would you do?

Self-Improvement Checklist for Spelling, Grammar, and Good Essay Writing

Count the number of times each of these was mentioned by the teacher or was corrected on your paper.

	Original	Rewritten	Difference
Misspellings	___	___	___
Awkward phrasing	___	___	___
Incorrect fact	___	___	___
Did not answer question	___	___	___
Too vague	___	___	___

After reviewing the essay checklist, I tried/will try to improve by taking the following steps:

If you could do this piece over, what would you do?
What do you want me to look for when I evaluate this piece? What questions do you have for me?

Self-Reflection Essay to Accompany a Completed Piece

As you write the essay, address the following items.

1. When I received this assignment my greatest worry was _____.
2. My worry turned out to be _____.
3. I found it easy/difficult to work with other people because ___.
4. I found that doing research was _____.
5. The biggest problem in doing research was ___.
6. If I had to do this research over I would ___.
7. Did the research get easier as I did more of it? Why? Why not?
8. The easiest part of the assignment was _____.
9. The hardest part of the assignment was _____.
10. What I learned about the topic that I did not know when I began was ____.

Reflection Prompts for Grading and Tests

- I think I deserve the above grade because

  _____.

- Students reflect on how they worked or behaved in a certain situation and then rate themselves by holding up 1, 2, 3, or 4 fingers (4 being the best). They then have to explain their rating and describe how they can get to the next applicable number (if they did not reach a 4).

- Questions to ask students before a test:
  - What grade do you think you will get on this test?

- How did you study for this test?
- How much time did you study?
- When did you study?

- Questions to have students ask themselves after taking a test:
  - How do I feel I did on the test?
  - Why was I successful or not successful?
  - What do I need to do to improve next time?
  - What do I need from the teacher to improve?

Multiple-Choice Test Self-Assessment

	Did not understand question/answers	Did not understand vocabulary	Read question carelessly	Did not know factual material
1.	___	___	___	___
2.	___	___	___	___
3.	___	___	___	___
4.	___	___	___	___
5.	___	___	___	___
6.	___	___	___	___
7.	___	___	___	___
8.	___	___	___	___
9.	___	___	___	___
10.	___	___	___	___
11.	___	___	___	___
12.	___	___	___	___
13.	___	___	___	___
14.	___	___	___	___
15.	___	___	___	___

Test topic: _____

Date taken: _____

Time spent studying: _____

Name of student: _____

Reflection Questions and Prompts for the Learning Process

- How did you approach your major project for the quarter? How did you schedule what you had to do? What did you do first, second, etc.?
- What part of the process was hard for you? What part was easy?
- Did you have enough support to begin and sustain your work?
- What makes learning *hard* for you? What makes learning *easy* for you?
- What are some things you are doing that are helping you learn in social studies?

- How do you generate ideas?
- How do you select the best work from among all your work? How do you know what is your best?
- What aspects of problem solving are difficult for you?
- How does sharing your work with others influence your choices?
- How do you react when someone suggests a change in your work?
- What do you do when you are too frustrated to go on?
- How can you tell when you are on the right track when you are writing?

Cooperative Group Process Assessment

On a scale of 1 to 5 (5 being the highest) rate your contribution to the group.

5   Very important contributions to all project components and in all phases of implementation; facilitated the work of others without taking over.

4   Significant contribution (made important suggestions and helped others in substantial ways; had an influential role in all project components).

3   Some contributions (made a few useful suggestions, helped other people with their research, problems, and contributed to the development of various project components; reminded others to keep working).

2   A minor contribution (made at least one useful suggestion, occasionally helped others, wasted little time, minor role in developing one or two different components of the project).

1   No real contribution (made no suggestions, did not help anyone, did little work, wasted time).

Circle your rating.   1   2   3   4   5

Briefly explain why you rate yourself as you do.

Rate each of the other people in your group and explain your ratings.

Reflection Prompts and Questions for Process Used to Develop Specific Work

- Where did you get your idea (ideas) for this piece?
- Did your topic emerge quickly?
- What kind of pre-writing preparation did you do?
- Why did you begin and end the piece this way?
- How did you go about doing this piece? What stages did you go through? What strategies did you follow? How long did it take you?
- Did you write fluently or in spurts? Explain.
- Did you reread what you wrote or just keep going?
- Did you run into any problems while you were working on this piece? If so, how did you deal with them?
- Did you share your work in process at some point? If so, how did that sharing influence what you ended up doing?
- Did you revise? If you wrote more than one draft, how did the paper change?
- Did you write for a particular audience? If you did have a particular audience in mind, did it make a difference to your writing?
- How did you know that you were on the right track as you were working on it?
- Did you accomplish what you set out to do? Explain.
- How did you know that the piece was finished?

Reflection Questions and Prompts for the Impact of Teaching on Students

- What is working about our method for learning vocabulary? Why? What is not working for you? Why?
- Is there anything else about your experience in class that you think I should know to help you learn better?
- What was helpful about how we structured the group project?
- What questions do you still have?
- How could I have presented the material to better suit your learning style?

Reflection Questions or Prompts Related to Goal Setting

- What would you like to learn more about in the next quarter?
- List three things you can do to improve your work in math.
- What do you need to do in the next marking period to become a better writer?

Reflective Science Essay

Describe the process you went through to conduct this investigation by addressing the following questions:

- How did you generate a hypothesis?
- How did you know it was testable?
- How did you come up with your experimental design?
- What problems did you have when you conducted the experiment?
- What could you have done differently to improve the experiment?

Appendix E:
Tools for
Action Research

Action Research Planning Module

Step 1: Identify the topics or ideas that your research may be related to.

Write down two or three ideas that you might act upon. You do not have to begin with a problem; you can begin with an idea about something that might be improved, or a desire to try an educational innovation, like the ones described in this book.

Think about the following questions as you brainstorm:
- What am I struggling with now? Why?
- What have I wanted to try? Why?
- What needs improvement and what might work?

Step 2: Describe the actions you will be taking and studying and articulate a rationale.

A. Review your ideas from Step 1 and select one idea to act upon. In choosing the idea you will work on, consider the following:
- How important is the idea to you? To your students?
- Is the idea manageable?
- Is it practical?

B. Write a working description of your intended action. Include the following:
- What is the specific action(s) you are planning?
- Who will be involved in the action?
- What do you need to implement the action(s)?

C. Write a rationale for your action. As you develop your rational, consider the following:
- Why are you choosing this action?
- Why is the action likely to improve the situation?
- How do your experiences or the reading that you have done relate?

Step 3: Write action research questions related to your actions.

A. What do you want to know about your idea and actions? Begin by writing all the questions that come to mind. Phrase your questions so that they include your actions.

B. Review your questions for recurring themes, overlap, and connections. Group the questions and revise them until they give as much guidance as possible. What seems to be the most important question? Which are subquestions?

Step 4: Create a plan for data collection.

Refer to the following list of various collection techniques to choose the ones that will be most helpful and valuable.

- journals/logs/diaries
- portfolios
- field notes
- questionnaires/surveys
- interaction schedules and checklists
- video-recording
- student work/performances
- anecdotal records
- document analysis
- interviews
- tape-recording
- photographs and slides

As you choose data collection techniques, consider the following questions:

- Will the techniques provide information related to the questions you've asked?
- Do the techniques have the potential to become automatic in your daily routine?
- Are the techniques ones that you can manage over time, given your work load?

Be sure that you collect data about your *actions* and the *results* of your actions.

Record your collection techniques here:

Step 5: Create a timetable to guide your research.

Think about the time you will need to carry out your action plan, to collect data, and to do the analysis and reflection. Be realistic. Allow time for reading, reflection, data analysis, feedback, and revision. Use the planning grid below or your own calendar to plan.

September

October

November

December

January

February

March

April

May

June

July

August

Source: Developed by Diane Cunningham. Copyright © 1998 by Learner-Centered Initiatives (LCI), Ltd.

Action Research Plan: Checklist for Quality

ACTION(S)—

_____ is/are focused on a problem, issue, or new practice.

_____ is/are classroom-based or connected to work responsibilities.

_____ is/are specifically described with reference to who is involved and how.

RATIONALE—

_____ is specific.

_____ references other's thinking and related literature.

QUESTION(S)—

_____ is/are specific enough to guide research.

_____ contain(s) the action being studied and relate(s) to the rationale.

_____ is/are phrased so that a yes/no answer is not possible.

DATA COLLECTION TECHNIQUES—

_____ will provide the information needed to answer the research questions.

_____ are manageable in terms of types and numbers.

_____ fit the researcher's style and routine—have the possibility of becoming automatic.

TIME PLAN—

_____ is realistic.

_____ allows time for reflection and analysis.

_____ allows time for feedback and revision.

Source: Developed by Diane Cunningham. Copyright © 1998 by Learner-Centered Initiatives (LCI), Ltd.

Rubric for an Action Research Plan

	Exemplary	Developed	Emerging	Undeveloped
ACTION RESEARCH PLAN How explicit and thoughtful is the action research plan?	The action research plan includes— • A specific description of the action(s) being taken and studied, with explanation of who is involved and how. • An explicit, detailed, and thorough rationale for the project that references other's thinking and related literature. • Specific, researchable questions that include the actions, relate to the rationale, and provide guidance for data collection and analysis. • A detailed list of realistic and manageable data collection techniques that will capture actions taken and results of actions. • A realistic and manageable timetable for collection, analysis, and write-up of data that allows time for revision and feedback.	The action research plan includes— • A specific description of the action(s) being taken and studied. • An explicit rationale for the project based on the researcher's personal experience. • Specific questions that include the researcher's actions, but could be refined to connect to the rationale to provide better guidance for data collection and analysis. • A detailed list of data collection techniques that will capture actions taken and results of actions but may be unmanageable given demands on the researcher's time and resources. • A specific timetable for collection, analysis, and write-up of data.	The action research plan includes— • A general description of the action being taken. • An implied rationale for the project. • Specific questions that reveal the researcher's area of interest but are not explicitly connected to actions being taken and need some refining to provide getter guidance for data collection and analysis. • Mention of data collection techniques, but no specific detail about what kind of data will be collected, when, or for what purpose. • A general mention of time needed to complete the project.	The action research plan— • Mentions the general area of focus, but actions being taken are unclear. • Needs a rationale. • Includes broad questions related to the general area but unconnected to any actions on the part of the researcher and too broad to guide research. • Lacks mention of specific techniques for gathering data. • Lacks a timetable to guide the project.

Source: Developed by Diane Cunningham. Copyright © 1998 by Learner-Centered Initiatives (LCI), Ltd.

References and Resources

Ackerman, D. B. (1989). Intellectual and practical criteria for successful curriculum integration. In H. H. Jacobs (Ed.), *Interdisciplinary curriculum: Design and implementation* (pp. 25–37). Alexandria, VA: Association for Supervision and Curriculum Development.

Aikin, W. (1942). *The story of the eight year study.* New York: Harper and Row.

Alberty, H. (1960). Core programs. In *Encyclopedia of educational research* (3rd ed., pp. 337–341). New York: Macmillan.

Beane, J. A. (1997). *Curriculum integration: Designing the core of democratic education.* New York: Teachers College Press.

Bissex, G. L., & Bullock, R. H. (Eds.). (1987). *Seeing for ourselves: Case study research by teachers of writing.* Portsmouth, NH: Heinemann.

Boyer, E. L. (1995). The educated person. In J. A. Beane (Ed.), *Toward a coherent curriculum: 1995 ASCD yearbook* (pp. 16–25). Alexandria, VA: Association for Supervision and Curriculum Development.

Brophy, J., & Alleman, J. (1991). A caveat: Curriculum integration isn't always a good idea. *Educational Leadership, 49*(2), 66.

Camp, R. (1992). Portfolio reflections in middle and secondary school classrooms. In K. B. Yancey (Ed.), *Portfolios in the writing classroom: An introduction* (pp. 61–79). Urbana, IL: National Council of Teachers of English.

Case, R. (1991). The anatomy of curricular integration. *Canadian Journal of Education, 16* (2), 215–224.

Center for the Study of Expertise in Teaching and Learning (CSETL). (1998). *Standards-based curriculum and assessment prototypes.* New York: Author.

Hanna, P. R., & Lang, A. D. (1950). Integration. In Walter S. Monroe (Ed.), *The encyclopedia of educational research* (pp. 592–600). New York: Macmillan.

Informal Committee of the Progressive Education Association on Evaluation of Newer Practices in Education. (1941). *New methods vs. old in American education.* New York: Bureau of Publications, Teachers College, Columbia University.

Jenkins, F. C. (1947). *The southern study: Cooperative study for the improvement of education.* Durham, NC: Duke University Press.

Kendall, J. S., & Marzano, R. J. (1996). *Content knowledge: A compendium of standards and benchmarks for k–12 education* (2nd ed.). Alexandria, VA: Association for Supervision and Curriculum Development (developed by Mid-continent Regional Educational Laboratory).

Kniep, W. (1979). Thematic units: Revitalizing a trusted tool. *The Clearinghouse on Global Education, 52,* 388–394.

Martin-Kniep, G., Cunningham, D., & Feige, D. M. (1998). *Why am I doing this? Purposeful teaching through portfolio assessment.* Portsmouth, NH: Heinemann.

Mickelson, J. M. (1957). What does research say about the effectiveness of the core curriculum? *School Review, 65,* 144–160.

Soodak, L. C., & Martin-Kniep, G. O. (1994). Authentic assessment and curriculum integration: Natural partners in need of thoughtful policy. *Educational Policy, 8(2),* 183–201.

Vars, G. F. (1996). The effects of interdisciplinary curriculum and instruction. In Peters S. Hlebowitsh & William G. Wraga (Eds.), *Annual review of research for school leaders, part II: Transcending traditional subject matter lines: Inter-disciplinary curriculum and instruction* (pp. 147–164). Reston, VA: National Association of Secondary School Principals.

Wrightstone, J. W. (1935). Evaluation of the integrated curriculum in the upper grades. *Elementary School Journal, 35,* 583–587.

Wrightstone, J. W. (1936). *Appraisal of experimental high school practices.* New York: Bureau of Publications, Teachers College, Columbia University.

Index

About the Authors

Giselle O. Martin-Kniep is the president of Learner-Centered Initiatives, Ltd., an educational consulting organization specializing in regional and school-based curriculum and assessment. Martin-Kniep has a strong background in organizational change, a doctorate in social sciences in education, and an Ed.S. degree in educational evaluation from Stanford University. From 1990 to 1995 she was a faculty member in the School of Education at Adelphi University. She has served as a program evaluator, a curriculum auditor, a researcher, and a teacher educator. Since 1990, she has worked with over 500 schools and districts both nationally and internationally in the areas of alternative assessment, integrated curriculum design, school change, and action research. She currently directs more than 35 comprehensive, multiyear regional and school-based national and international professional development programs for K–12 teachers. She also works as a consultant for the International Baccalaureate and the New York State Department of Education. In addition, she is president and CEO of the Center for the Study of Expertise in Teaching and Learning.

Martin-Kniep has written numerous books, chapters in edited texts, and articles. Her two most recent publications are *Why Am I Doing This? Purposeful Teaching Through Portfolio Assessment* (Heinemann, 1998) *and Capturing the Wisdom of Practice: Portfolios for Teachers and Administrators* (ASCD, 1999). She may be reached at Learner-Centered Initiatives, Ltd., 20 Elm Place, Sea Cliff, NY 11579; telephone: 516-794-4694. E-mail: gmklci@aol.com

Diane Cunningham (author of Chapter 8, "Action Research: Asking and Answering Questions About Practice") is an educational consultant for Learner-Centered Initiatives. Over the past 12 years she has engaged in various action research projects and has guided many teachers and administrators in carrying out action research. She coauthored a chapter on authentic assessment and is co-editor of *Why Am I Doing This? Purposeful Teaching Through Portfolio Assessment*. She may be reached at Learner-Centered Initiatives, Ltd., 20 Elm Place, Sea Cliff, NY 11579; telephone: 516-794-4694. E-mail: dianelci@hofflink.com